Teaching Tools

for

the 21st Century

By
Carolyn Coil

Pieces of Learning

CLC0200
ISBN 1-880505-55-X
© 1997 Carolyn Coil
Cover Design by John Steele

Table of Contents

Introduction

DEDICATION

With special love to:

My parents, William and Charlotte Hendrix, who have always supported me and cheered me on in anything I have attempted to do.

Two childhood friends, Mary Baber Olsson of Chicago, Illinois and Kathy Brown Hudson of St. Augustine, Florida who shared all of my school years with me and are still two of my closest friends today.

Mary C. (Kitty) Walker, the very special teacher who inspired, motivated, loved and encouraged me throughout my junior high years and who continues to be an important person in my life.

ACKNOWLEDGMENTS

Special thanks to all the educators who have used the ideas presented in this book and have given me feedback about what worked best and how to make some of my "tools" function better.

Thanks to my friends Joan Shipps, Dian Pizurie, and Mona Livermont who helped me with the list of movies and videos about teachers.

Thanks to Pieces of Learning staff Kathy Balsamo, Nancy Johnson, Pat Bleidorn and Stan Balsamo for their suggestions, assistance and encouragement.

INTRODUCTION

How to Use This Book

As I travel around the country doing workshops for teachers, I notice several theories, ideas and buzz words. *Learning styles, multiple intelligences, cultural diversity, inclusion, student directed learning, new technologies, alternative assessment* are some of the words I hear. As I researched these ideas and concepts, I realized how powerful they are in the potential they hold to change the whole face of education. At the same time I realize that most teachers feel overwhelmed with the number of theories and changes they need to absorb. I know they need tools to help them and make their enormous task easier.

A *tool* can be defined as *any instrument or device that is used to make the work of one's profession or occupation easier, more effective or more efficient.* Teachers have always used a variety of tools, from the slate and chalkboard to the personal computer. Teaching tools also include plan books, curriculum designs, and visual organizers.

However, I feel it is important to create tools to help teachers incorporate the *new* educational theories and ideas and use them in their classrooms. These tools will help teachers facilitate the learning of their students into the 21st century.

Many teaching tools are presented in this book. As you read, I'll introduce you to these tools and will show examples of how to use each. You will find flexible strategies and techniques for incorporating learning styles and modalities, multiple intelligences, and Bloom's taxonomy. You will find tools to help you understand and manage cultural diversity, conflict, and the inclusion of special needs and gifted students. There is a chapter about assessment and one about technology. Each contains practical information to help teachers now!

Tools for Reflective Learning

Because of the amount and variety of information presented in this book, it is best to read the *Questions to Consider* box you will find at the beginning of each chapter. These are the ideas that I will discuss in the chapter.

Then read a section or the chapter. The *Reflections* box reviews the main concepts presented in the chapter.

I have included two other tools - one-page reproducible pages recognizable by their shadows - and you will find *Teacher Reflection Pages* throughout the book. These reflection pages are content specific. For each topic discussed in the book, a *Reflection Page* offers questions for reflection and discussion. You may use these pages individually or as part of a teacher self-assessment portfolio; their best use will be in a small group setting. They can guide reflective thinking about a particular topic in various group settings:

- ✓ University classes
- ✓ Site based management teams
- ✓ Collaborative groups and teams
- ✓ Grade level or subject area planning meetings
- ✓ Faculty meetings
- ✓ Coaching/collegial support teams
- ✓ Beginning teacher programs
- ✓ Staff development sessions

Another tool to use in reflective thinking is the *Coil 4-I Planning Model*™. Use the reproducible form of the model on page 7. This is a generic planning model that you can use individually or in any group planning session. I often use it in my workshops to help participants structure their thinking and planning in implementing workshop ideas.

Use the *4-I Planning Model*™ any time you are introduced to new concepts, thoughts or theories. This can be when you listen to a speaker, when you are in conversation with a colleague, when you are part of a decision-making team, or when you are reading or studying on your own. This tool will help you understand what is being taught or discussed and gives you a way to apply new concepts to your own situation. This model has four parts (4-I's): *Imagination, Ideas, Information,* and *Implementation.*

1. ***Imagination*** Use this part of the model to capture any of the thoughts that may go through your head while you are reading or hearing about a new idea or concept. Include visions and dreams that may or may not become solid ideas. Our brains constantly have imaginings running through them! Capture them on paper as you read and listen, for they are generally the best source of new ideas.

2. ***Ideas*** Ideas are more solid than imaginings. When you get an idea, you usually think: "This is how I could do it" or "It could work like this!" Write your ideas in the second section of the *4-I Planning Model*™.

3. ***Information*** When you have an idea, most of the time you need to gather more information to see how it might be useful in your particular situation. Write down the type of information you need and where you might find it. The information gathering phase is important, but it is also the step in the *4-I Planning Model*™ where groups or individuals have difficulty. Beware of always needing to gather more and more information before you take any action. Sometimes we spend so much time gathering information about a new idea that the idea itself gets lost and you never implement it!

4. ***Implementation*** This is the most important part of the model, for it is the action step where change takes place. For a new idea to have any long-term worth, you must implement it. In the *4-I Planning Model*™, write an implementation plan with target dates and agree upon it. Modify the plan as you gather information.

Model

COIL "4-I" PLANNING MODEL

Imagination
(Visions - Possibilities - Brainstorms)

Ideas
(It could happen like this . . . This is how we could do it)

Information
(All of the things we need to find out
concerning our situation and the possibilities we see)

Implementation
(The plan for turning our ideas into reality)

Chapter 1

Teaching Creatively in the 21st Century

Questions to Consider

1. What new skills will my students need to meet the changes of the 21st century?

2. What are the essential keys for teaching and learning in the 21st century?

3. What place does "choice" — teacher and student — play in learning?

4. Where can I find a practical lesson planning format that will help me individualize for my students?

A Time of Rapid Change

Recently I spent time in England. Everywhere I looked, I could see the new juxtaposed upon the old, evidence of centuries upon centuries of continual change. Nowhere was this more apparent than in the city of York, a city located in the industrial heartland of England, halfway between London to the South and Edinburgh to the North. The Romans settled this city in the Bronze Age in 71 A.D. Measured by American standards, it is a city with a long history and is a city that has experienced wave upon wave of change. As I walked through York, I could see Roman ruins alongside artifacts from the Saxon invasion. I could see portions of a medieval castle and was able to walk on top of the city wall built in the Middle Ages. I ate a meal in a pub built at the time of the American Revolution during the reign of King George III.

Besides these historic things, York has something very special — something that symbolized the whole idea of CHANGE for me when I saw it. In 1984, a group of developers decided to build a modern shopping mall in York. They chose the site carefully in an area of dilapidated buildings not far from the center of town on a street called Coppergate.

When they bulldozed the buildings and started digging through the layers of earth underneath, they discovered a completely preserved Viking village. Mud and dirt buried it beneath Coppergate for centuries. Archaeologists were called in and they discovered layer upon layer of well-preserved archaeological artifacts. These layers, seen in an underground exhibit, are a visual representation of change. I looked at a section of the earth and saw physical evidence of the civilizations that had existed on that spot from the Bronze Age to the present. And yes, on top of that, there is a brand new shopping mall!

I like what they've done in York, not because I love shopping malls, but because they've looked forward as well as looking backward. They have not destroyed the past, but they aren't stuck in it either.

So often educators take a "rear view mirror" approach. We approach the educational process the way we drive after we've been picked up on radar going too fast. We put most of our attention into looking backwards to see where we've been and then try to do the things that worked five years ago or 10 years ago or even a generation ago.

As we come into the 21st century, we need to spend less time looking out the rear view mirror and more time looking at the road ahead. Change has always been part of the human condition, but never has change been so rapid as it has been in this last decade of the 20th century. Sometimes change comes at such a fast pace that it's difficult to keep up with it all! The one thing that seems certain is that we will continue to experience this rapid change throughout the 21st century.

Linking School to the 21st Century World of Work

Like other areas of life, the world of work is changing. Automated and advanced technologies are replacing many of our traditional unskilled and semiskilled workers. Jobs now require more advanced technical skills, but often our students do not have the relevant skills they need to work effectively now or in the 21st century.

Unskilled labor is no longer a valuable economic commodity, and it will become even less so in the years to come. It is widely believed that by the turn of the century, the unskilled person will be virtually unemployable in most of the industrialized world. Consider these facts:

According to Willard Daggett, Director of the International Center for Leadership in Education, in 1950, 60% of all jobs were unskilled and most paid a middle class wage. In 1994, 33% of all jobs were unskilled and most were low paying. It is predicted that by the year 2000, only 15% of jobs will be unskilled and nearly all will pay only the minimum wage. If students never do technical reading and writing in school, never work in teams, don't develop

the ability to judge quality work and effort, don't develop a work ethic and don't understand economics and the business world, they will have problems in the world of work. [1]

One role of education is to prepare students for this world of work. We need to prepare our students to do the type of jobs that will be available in the 21st century. However, the business world expresses much concern about the transfer of school-based skills into the workplace setting.

Agriculture no longer dominates the American economy as it did when the 20th century dawned. Most of those who continue to work in agriculture in the 21st century will need advanced technological, financial and organizational skills. Manufacturing no longer requires workers who do routine tasks again and again. Instead, we have shifted to a more flexible and automated manufacturing system. The result is that industrial workers need technological skills and the ability to process information symbolically, mostly via computers. They also need advanced reading and language skills and the ability to think critically.

Workers in the 21st century will deal mostly with services and information. To do this, they will need to understand advanced technological applications involving the use of math, language and thinking skills. Knowledge of statistics, logic, probability and measurement systems, and applied physics will be the norm. Because they will need to communicate with customers regularly, these same workers will also need to express themselves well, organize information and activities, and do a great deal of technical reading and writing.

Furthermore, they will need to work well in task-oriented groups or teams and solve problems critically and creatively. However, for the most part, schools teach students to work independently, while the world of work needs workers who know how to work interdependently with one another. Because they will be part of a global economy and multicultural workplace, this interdependence also involves the ability to understand people from a variety of cultures who may have different cultural values and norms.

Other Needs of 21st Century Students

As important as they are, future jobs and the world of work should not be our only considerations as we think of the needs of the 21st century student. Job preparation is only one of many needs our students have. We also must consider their abilities to be good citizens, contributing family members, lifelong learners, appreciators of the arts, history, and culture, and caring, compassionate people. The teacher holds the key to developing these more intangible educational outcomes.

Three Keys for Teaching in the 21st Century

Three essential keys for successful teaching and learning in the 21st century are *Flexibility, Choices,* and *Planning.* Each of these key ideas moves away from the 19th and 20th century Industrial Age mode of everyone learning and doing the same thing at the same time—to the Information Age model of individualized lifelong learning. If we want our children to develop abilities in higher level thinking,

teachers must model teaching in ways that enhance critical and creative thought.

Flexibility

As we approach the 21st century, we can no longer continue to give all students the same assignment and expect them to complete it simultaneously with equal accuracy and quality. A "one size fits all" lesson usually fits no one! Flexibility implies that all students will not, together in a lockstep fashion, do classroom activities and assignments chosen by the teacher. Flexibility means acknow- ledging that it will take some students a long time to learn an idea or skill while other students already know it before you begin the lesson. And it means making provisions for these differing ability levels within your classroom.

Flexible teachers must be willing to give up some of their lecture time and use texts and workbooks as just one of many classroom resources. A flexible teacher realizes that doing a series of questions at the end of the chapter does not meet most students' learning needs.

Flexibility means allowing for differences in such things as:

- ✓ Learning styles
- ✓ Learning modalities
- ✓ Strengths/weaknesses in the multiple intelligences
- ✓ Pace of learning and lesson presentation
- ✓ Time needed to complete a task
- ✓ Student interests
- ✓ Ability levels

Through technology many of our students can now access new information with the press of a button. For example, 10 years ago students who were assigned to write a report on the explorations of

Christopher Columbus would get several books, research the information, and write the report by hand. Now they can access a multitude of sources on CD ROM and the Internet, cut and paste the information electronically, press a computer key and print out their report. As we approach the 21st century, our assignments must require much more thinking than that!

Due to technological advances and the greater availability of information from a multitude of sources, students have an unlimited access to knowledge. No longer is a teacher the only resource for knowledge and information. The role of the teacher is changing, with the teacher becoming a model of lifelong learning for his or her students. Thus, students and their teachers are all fellow learners who can find new information and share this information with one another.

Yet, technology can also drown us in a flood of information. Our students can end up spending all their time just trying to sift through the vast amount of information that is readily available. Teachers, too, have limited instructional time. When the curriculum is merely added to with more and more "stuff," teachers struggle and realize they cannot do it all. There needs to be another approach.

Teachers do not need to know all the answers. This is really an advantage educationally, because when teachers don't know the answers, they can model what learning is all about. Teachers become learners as well as their students, assuming the role of co-learner in the classroom. As we approach the 21st century, this role for teachers is becoming more and more necessary.

With so much knowledge and information, how do we know what should be taught? One approach, called "selective abandonment" by Art Costa, is to remove outdated, irrelevant and unnecessary information from the curriculum. Teachers need to do this regularly. Consider it cleaning out your mental file cabinet! Even when they do this, most teachers are overwhelmed at all they are required to teach. One of the best approaches to flexible teaching is to integrate and connect the curriculum through thematic interdisciplinary units.

Choices

Student Choices / Student-Directed Learning

Choices are everywhere. Consider an average day for eleven year old Richard. He goes to a video store and selects a video from 1000s of titles available. Next, he strolls through the mall looking for a new shirt and can choose from the hundreds of different shirts on the clothing racks in every store he passes. Later he goes to the grocery store with his mom. He doesn't even think about the number of cereals or soft drinks he chooses from as he fills the shopping cart with his favorite foods. Choices fill our students' everyday lives.

Choice affects education like all other goods and services in our advanced modern economy. Schools in the 21st century will market themselves and attempt to satisfy the expectations of their clients—the parents and students. Within the classroom, students need to have choices in their learning as well. Structure many choices into each student's day. Why is this important? Students feel a sense of ownership in the tasks they are to do when teachers give choices in classroom assignments. When teachers include the element of choice in learning experiences, they increase the chances that students will achieve optimal learning.

As you plan thematic interdisciplinary units, and when you plan lessons and learning activities for your students each week and each day, ask yourself these questions:

✓ Why am I teaching this?
✓ Why is it important for my students to do this activity?
✓ How can I eliminate some redundant or rote activities and still meet the same educational objectives and competencies?
✓ How can I structure this unit or lesson in such a way to give my students choices?

These questions will help plan and determine the educational outcomes and competencies our students need, the future citizens of the 21st century. It is important to remember that what goes on in the classroom affects what students learn. This is the area where teachers have the most control. One way to affect student progress in learning is to offer choices in learning activities. Let's now look further at the idea of giving choices in learning.

Types of Student Choices

For most students, there have been few times in their school lives that teachers have allowed them to make choices. This situation is rapidly changing as we approach the 21st century. Constructive choices for students come in all shapes and sizes. Students should be able to choose which tasks to do to accomplish goals and mandated outcomes. The teacher needs to extend multiple choices for students by varying the structure of the curriculum, classroom activities, and projects.

The number and types of student choices depend on the teacher's comfort level with a variety of instructional approaches. Students should be able to use a variety of approaches for the same task.

Give them choices in activities, timing, and/or ways to learn. These choices must be real choices, with no hidden preference by the teacher. Eventually, give students who become adept at making choices for their own learning the opportunity to develop their own choices and alternatives.

Giving students choices is risky. Student-directed learning requires a tremendous shift in the way teachers think and how they plan. Teachers have to be flexible because once students make choices, they don't always make the choices or go in directions teachers think they should.

A word of caution is necessary. We don't want to give our students so much choice that they end up learning nothing. The role of the teacher is to plan and structure the curriculum to meet essential outcomes and essential competencies to achieve student excellence. For these reasons, the teacher must be the one to outline the parameters and opportunities for choice.

Advantages of Student Choices

Allowing students to direct their own learning has several advantages:

✓ Students learn good decision making skills.
✓ Students help establish rules for classroom management.
✓ Students can and do take ownership of their learning.
✓ The curriculum can be adapted to meet student interests.
✓ Lessons are more meaningful and students become personally involved in them.
✓ Teachers are able to narrow the focus of curriculum units.

The best way to give students choices is to allow them choices within a range of potential objectives, activities and outcomes. A student's learning style, learning modality, individual interests and use of the various intelligences will determine the student choices in meeting the objectives.

Teacher Choices/Teacher-Directed Learning

In a classroom where students direct their own learning by making choices in curricular activities, the teacher becomes valuable as an experienced guide in the process of learning. Teachers need to take on the role of guides in the classroom because deciding what content should be learned or studied is very difficult. Students need guidance to assess what they need to learn so they can solve a problem or complete a project.

Providing such guidance can prove challenging for teachers who must also ensure that students meet academic objectives and mandates established by school districts or states. Many states list objectives in the state's curriculum framework and give students standardized tests to make sure they meet these standards. In some school districts, severe penalties can result if students fall below certain percentiles on standardized tests.

Because of this, one valid concern in giving students choices in their learning is that standards will not be met because there will be too many gaps in students' knowledge. Teachers or their superiors may feel that the only way to ensure that this does not happen is to have everyone cover certain books, topics or assignments. Yet meeting standards can work hand in hand with student-directed learning when teachers guide student choice

making. The choice comes in HOW to meet the standards, not in whether or not the standards will be met.

Many teachers are frustrated and confused, wanting to be flexible and give students choices in their learning activities yet feeling pressure to make sure students meet district or statewide standards. These two ideas do not have to be mutually exclusive, but accomplishing both takes planning! Let's now look at the third key for successful teaching in the 21st century — Planning.

Planning

While agreeing in principle that learning should be flexible and provide choices, many teachers have done little in these areas because of the vast amount of planning they perceive it requires. In fact, it does take planning to reach differing ability levels and a variety of interest areas.

Look at the *Individual Student Lesson Plan* format on page 15. It is an effective, easy-to-use tool for lesson planning which will help you be flexible. It gives you a structure to provide for student choices, yet also allows you to include required teacher-choice learning activities for all students. This format is one of several *Individual Student Lesson Plan* formats you will find in this book. In the remaining portion of this chapter and in several subsequent chapters, you will discover how you can use this tool to plan choices in learning for your students.

How to Begin

Some teachers teach using interdisciplinary thematic units, while others are more content or subject based. An interdisciplinary thematic unit uses a topic or concept as a theme and infuses this theme into a number of different content areas. A content-based or subject-based unit may touch on other disciplines, but its focus is on one subject area. You can use the *Individual Student Lesson Plan* format with both.

Begin planning your unit by generating a list of broad unit questions, objectives and outcomes. (A sample is found on page 16.) Then brainstorm as many activities as possible that students could do to answer the questions and accomplish these outcomes. (See page 18.) You may want to collaborate with other teachers as you gather ideas for activities and look at a variety of resources about the topic. Be sure to ask your students what they already know or are interested in about the topic or subject you will be focusing on. Brainstorming potential unit activities with your students is a very important element of lesson planning.

Using a visual organizer helps in structuring your planning as you begin to think of the various activities students could do to answer the major unit questions. Look at the examples that show questions about *Inventors and Inventions* and note the development of student activities based on one of these questions. Reproducible forms are also included in this chapter for you to use in planning your own questions, lessons, and units.

NOTES

"When we do the best that we can, we never know what miracle is wrought in our life or in the life of another."

Helen Keller

INDIVIDUAL LESSON PLAN - Subject Activities

	Required Activities Teacher's Choice	Product/Performance Required	Assessment Required Activities

	Student Choices in Ways to Learn	Product/Performance Student Choice	Assessment Student Choice
Optional Student-Parent Cooperative Activity	Science Social Studies Performing Arts Language Arts Visual Arts Math		

ACTIVITIES - STUDENT CHOICES

Science	Language Arts

Social Studies	Visual Arts

Performing Arts	Math

©1997 Carolyn Coil and Pieces of Learning

Inventors and Inventions

What do I want my students to know about this topic?
What are the major questions we need to ask about the topic?

Who were some famous inventors?

What were their inventions?

What effect have inventions had on modern life?

What are some inventions students would like to see in the future?

How was the transition from the Agricultural Age to the Industrial Age similar to
the transition we are going through from the Industrial Age to the Information Age?

How do different inventions work?

What are the various parts of inventions and their functions?

What stages do inventions go through before they are useful? Do they change with time?

What is the difference between an invention and a discovery?

How could I invent something totally new?

Do you have to be a genius to be an inventor?

How do you get a patent for something you have invented?

Do new inventions make life easier or more difficult?

What new things have been invented since my students were born? Since
their parents were born?

Are many inventions similar to one another?

What happens when inventions are failures?

Lesson or Thematic Unit

What do I want my students to know about this topic?
What are the major questions we need to ask about the topic?

* _____
   _____

* _____
   _____

* _____
   _____

* _____
   _____

* _____
   _____

* _____
   _____

* _____
   _____

* _____
   _____

Sample Planner for Curriculum Development

Take one of the questions and consider the various types of activities students might be able to do to answer the question. In planning a unit, do this for each question.

Who were some famous inventors?

Possible Student Activities	Student Product
Cut out a full-sized person from butcher paper. Make him a famous inventor. Write about him in the cutout.	Butcher paper person
Invent a 3-dimensional game about inventors.	3-D game
Read about several inventors. Identify common characteristics and report to your class. Use visuals.	Report with visuals
Read a biography about a famous inventor. Dress as this inventor and give an oral report to the class.	Oral report
Read the textbook pages about inventors. Outline or make a web of the information.	Outline or web
Listen to a talk by a local inventor. Write a reaction paper.	Reaction paper
Write a dialogue between two famous inventors who lived during different periods of history.	Dialogue
Make a diorama showing a failure a famous inventor experienced.	Diorama
Produce a radio talk show on audio tape. Interview a famous inventor.	Radio talk show
Pretend you are a famous inventor. Demonstrate your favorite invention.	Demonstration
Compose a song about an inventor. Sing it to the class or make a video of it MTV style.	Song or musical video
Make a collage showing famous inventors and their inventions.	Collage
Write a poem from the point of view of a famous inventor.	Poem

Sample Planner for Curriculum Development

Take one of the questions and consider the various types of activities students might be able to do to answer the question. In planning a unit, you should do this for each question.

_____

(Question)

Possible Student Activities	Student Product
1.	
2.	
3.	
4.	
5.	
6.	
7.	
8.	
9.	

Using the Individual Student Lesson Plan Format

After you have done this initial planning of your unit, you should be ready to use the *Individual Student Lesson Plan* format. Decide first which activities you want all of your students to do. List these activities in the block in the center labeled *Required Activities - Teacher's Choice*. The products that will be turned in as a result of doing these activities and criteria for assessment will be listed in the two blocks on the right. Look at an example from the *Inventors and Inventions* unit:

In addition to outlining the teacher required activities for all students, the *Individual Stu-*

Required Activities Teacher's Choice	Product/Performance	Assessment
1. Read the textbook information about inventions in both the social studies and science books. Make a Compare / Contrast chart showing the information.	1. Compare/Contrast chart	1. Appropriate visual Correct facts Deductive reasoning Organization
2. Listen to a talk by a local inventor. Write a reaction paper.	2. Reaction paper	2. Facts & opinions clearly stated Sentence structure
3. Take a final test about Inventors & Inventions.	3. Test answers	3. Accurate answers Numerical score

dent Lesson Plan format also provides a structured method whereby students can make choices in their learning activities. It gives teachers the flexibility to individualize and serve a variety of subject areas, learning styles, learning modalities, taxonomy levels and/or ability levels. Let's take a look at one set of student choice activities from the *Inventors and Inventions* unit. In the example I have organized the student choices according to subject areas.

If you look back at the sample *Individual Student Lesson Plan* format you will see there are blocks indicating key learning areas. Use these for student choice activities. Other versions of the *Individual Student Lesson Plan* format found in upcoming chapters of this book have one block for each of four learning styles (pages 33-34), four learning modalities (pages 42-43), and six taxonomy levels (pages 54-57). In general, three activity choices should be listed in each block for students in grade 4 or higher. Younger students do better with fewer choices in each block.

INDIVIDUAL LESSON PLAN - Subject Activities

Assessment / Required Activities	Product/Performance / Required	Required Activities / Teacher's Choice
		Each subject area teacher could require specific activities that would be recorded in this space.

Optional Student-Parent Cooperative Activity

(16) Calculate the percentage of time per day you use 10 inventions.

Student Choices in Ways to Learn

Science — 2
Social Studies — 6
Performing Arts — 7
Language Arts — 10
Visual Arts — 15
Math — 17

Product/Performance / Student Choice

2. Time line
6. Chart
7. Monologue
10. Letter
15. Mural
17. Graph

Assessment / Student Choice

2. Chronological major stages included
6. Clarity; major inventions included
7. Creativity; factual information
10. Logical reasons; grammatically correct; sentence structure
15. Artistic quality; creativity; originality
17. Clarity of graph; accuracy of information

©1997 Carolyn Coil and Pieces of Learning

ACTIVITIES - STUDENT CHOICES

Science

1. Design your car of the future. Explain how it would work.
2. Develop a time line showing the stages in the development of the telephone.
3. Draw a diagram showing how the invention of your choice works.

Language Arts

10. Write a letter to the editor thanking Gutenberg for inventing the printing press.
11. Make a crossword puzzle of inventions.
12. Explain the difference between an invention and a discovery. Give examples.

Social Studies

4. Research the life of a famous inventor. Share your information with your class in a creative way.
5. Do a skit showing the changes brought about by a specific invention.
6. Make a chart showing major inventions of World War II.

Visual Arts

13. Create a collage of 19th century or 20th century inventions.
14. Invent a hat that does something for you. Draw and label the hat.
15. With a group of classmates, paint a mural of inventions.

Performing Arts

7. Write & perform a monologue pretending you are a famous inventor.
8. Pretend you are an invention. Act out what you are. Your classmates are allowed 20 questions to guess what you are.
9. Write and perform a song about an invention.

Math

16. Calculate the % of time per day that you use any 10 inventions.
17. Survey your neighborhood to see what cars people own. Show car ownership on a graph.
18. Write a report explaining how math was used to help develop an invention.

How Student Choices Can Be Structured and Implemented

The *Individual Student Lesson Plan* format allows the teacher to have some control over the activities the students are doing, using the required teacher choice activities and by the way the student choice activities are implemented. For example, students could be told to choose two activities from one of the student choice blocks and one from another. Or one from each block, or two from two different blocks. It is up to each teacher to decide how to structure the choices.

When using the *Individual Student Lesson Plan* format there also needs to be some type of a time line or schedule so that students, their parents and the teacher know the date various products and assignments must be turned in.

Give each student a copy of the *Individual Student Lesson Plan* format with the *Teacher's Choice* and *Student Choice* activities already filled in. When the new unit is introduced, review all the activities and choices with the entire class. Next each student makes his or her choice of activities by writing the number for each activity on the line in the center block. Then the student writes on the chart what products and/or performances are required for each activity that he or she has chosen. Finally, the criteria for assessing each individual activity is recorded. For more on assessment and evaluation, see Chapter 6.

The *Individual Student Lesson Plan* format for Inventors and Inventions is on page 21. Use the reproducible blank format with student choices by subject area on page 14 to design your own units.

Using the Individual Student Lesson Plan format in a Mixed Ability Classroom

In a mixed ability classroom, use this format for everyone. Structure it with easier choices and more difficult choices, or if you prefer that all students have the same choices, differentiate the quality, level and expectations for the products depending on the ability level of each child. Teacher guidance is needed to make sure students make appropriate choices and that they know how to approach the task once the choice is made. See page 94 about developing Questivities™ to learn more about guiding students' thinking after they have chosen an activity.

Gifted and high ability students often finish their work before others in the class. When this happens while they are working on activities from the *Individual Student Lesson Plan* format, they do not have to sit around and wait for others to finish, nor do they have to do "busy work." They can either choose an additional activity from the choices in the lesson plan format or think of a new activity about the topic as an additional choice.

Adapting the Individual Student Lesson Plan format for primary students

Primary students need to learn to make choices, but the choices need to be fewer and completed over a shorter period of time. Use a bulletin board to show student choices and have students put their names on the bulletin board next to the activity they choose. A good way to begin is to have a total of four student choice activities and have each student choose one.

Using the Individual Student Lesson Plan format to form student groups

Use an Activity Chart to record the activities that each of your students choose. (See sample on page 24.) Each student choice activity is numbered and can be easily checked off under the student's name. When all the student choices have been recorded on this chart, you have a visual organizer which you can use to group students according to the activities they choose. Some of the activities may need to be done in a group (such as a skit) but even students doing individual activities will benefit by planning, discussing and brainstorming with others who are doing the same activity.

Using the Optional Student-Parent Cooperative Activity

Many parents become interested in their child's school projects. To capture this interest and use it in a positive way, you may wish to let your students choose one activity to do with their parents. This not only involves the parents in the activities of the school, it also helps them model as lifelong learners for their children. For overly zealous parents who always want to help their child, this provides an outlet to do it!

Reflections

* 21st Century students will need a multiplicity of new skills to meet the needs and demands of a rapidly changing world.

* Three essential keys for teaching and learning in the 21st century are *flexibility*, *choices*, and *planning*.

* We need to offer opportunities for students to make choices and direct their own learning in combination with required teachers' choice learning activities.

* The *Individual Student Lesson Plan* format provides a structure for planning and implementing both types of learning activities.

[1]Educational Leadership, Volume 52, Number 8, May 1995. P. 46

Activity Chart

Students' Names

Student Choice Activities	Alicia	Carlos	Danielle	Evan	Edwardo	Gina	Heather	Jim	Kara	Maria	Mark	Nathan	Ophra	Paul	Pedro	Quintan	Rachel	Rusty	Sarah	Taneka	Tom
1			✔					✔			✔								✔		✔
2	✔				✔									✔						✔	
3				✔			✔														
4		✔		✔									✔			✔		✔			✔
5						✔				✔							✔				
6			✔				✔				✔			✔							
7		✔					✔											✔			
8				✔						✔					✔					✔	
9	✔									✔											
10					✔					✔			✔				✔				✔
11								✔													
12									✔			✔			✔						
13					✔				✔		✔		✔					✔			
14					✔	✔	✔						✔							✔	
15	✔		✔									✔					✔				
16					✔																
17					✔			✔							✔			✔			
18		✔												✔							

This group of students was instructed to make 3 choices from the 18 student choice activities available. Each child's choices are recorded.

Students who chose 5 and 15, group activities, were grouped together. Other potential groupings were Edwardo, Maria, Ophra, Rachel and Tom to work in a group on activity 10. By using Questivities™ (page 94) to guide them, these flexible groupings of students were able to work very effectively.

Activity Chart

Students' Names

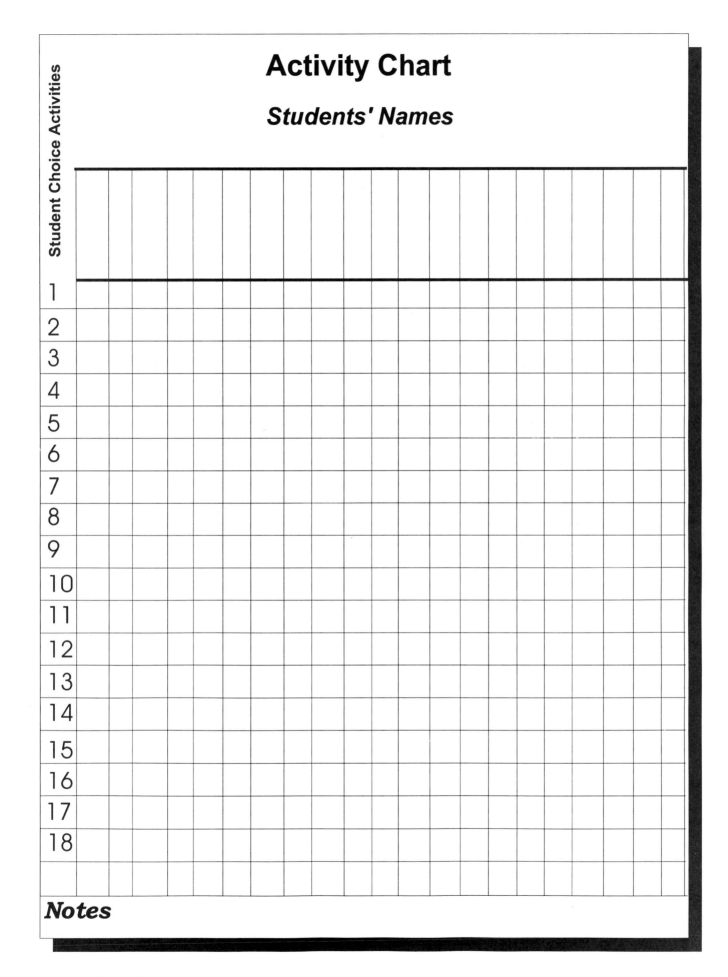

Student Choice Activities

1
2
3
4
5
6
7
8
9
10
11
12
13
14
15
16
17
18

Notes

Chapter 2

Learning Styles

Questions to Consider

1. What do learning styles indicate?

2. What are the kinds of learning styles?

3. Why is it important for students to know their strong and weak styles?

4. How can I accommodate all learning styles into the curriculum?

Teachers in the 21st century will need working knowledge of basic learning styles. It is important to know about these styles and be able to work with each so that you can plan your lessons taking each style into account. In the past, good teachers have intuitively used a variety of teaching styles. But as we enter the 21st century, we must be more intentional about how we are teaching. We no longer have the luxury of ignoring or refusing to teach to any of these styles.

Successful adults can generally work in any learning style, but most have a style of preference and strength. In the same way, it is equally important for you to help your students to identify their strong and weak style(s). Over time assist them in becoming adept at working in all styles. It would not be good teaching practice to identify the preferred learning style for each of our students and then restrict them to that style! When students are encouraged to develop a learning style they previously considered weak, rather than detracting from other areas, the develop-ment seems to create a synergistic effect in which all areas of mental performance improve.

Learning styles indicate the ways in which people process information. Dr. Anthony Gregorc has identified four basic learning styles. They are:

Concrete Sequential
Abstract Sequential
Concrete Random
Abstract Random

Both of the **concrete** styles deal with objects and concrete, hands-on, experiential learning.

Both of the **abstract** styles deal with more theoretical thinking apart from one object or example.

Both of the **sequential** styles deal with processing information in a linear, orderly fashion.

Both of the **random** styles deal with processing information in no particular order, in a more haphazard, non-uniform way.

Research studies by Griggs & Dunn (1984) show a positive relationship between academic achievement, beneficial attitudes, and desirable classroom behavior and the accommodation of students' learning style preferences in the classroom.[2] Thus it is important for you to discover the learning styles of your students. As you read the next several pages, think about your own students. Which students fit the descriptions of each learning style?

The Concrete Sequential Learning Style

Jana is in the 4th grade and is considered an excellent student. She has her school supplies on the first day of school and generally keeps them intact all year. She writes down her assignments, turns them in on time and (to the chagrin of other students) reminds the teacher when they are due. Her outlines are always done in sequential order, with the proper Roman numerals and letters. However, she is not an imaginative student and seems to lack creativity. She dislikes teachers who skip around in the book or who don't teach in a logical order. Her preferred learning style is concrete sequential. Schools usually reward concrete sequential students.

This student likes to:

• read and follow directions. For example, this student will read the directions before touching an electronic device or follow the recipe exactly when cooking something.

• take notes, make charts and create outlines. This student is the one other students turn to for the notes to study before a major test.

• participate in "hands-on" experiences, including pencil and paper exercises. As the name of this learning style suggests, this student likes to work with concrete things and does well with written work, hands-on projects, and assignments involving specific products.

• have an organized teacher. This student will still have the syllabus on the last day of the term and will know if you've stuck to it!

• always know what the marking system is. This student can tell you exactly what grades he or she has made on each assignment since the beginning of the grading period. If the teacher forgets to return a set of papers, this student will remind her to do it.

The Abstract Sequential Learning Style

Colin, an 11th grader, has always liked to read. He began reading when he was three, and it seems he has had a book in his hands ever since! By the time he was in first grade he was reading at a fourth grade level. He is very good at math and science and looks at everything logically. Colin can win arguments with anyone if only logic is involved. His intuitive and social skills are not as well developed. He has a hard time with his peers and some of the other kids call him a 'nerd'. He has a crush on an 11th grade girl and has thought through all the steps to ask her to the prom. He's sure if he approaches this situation in a logical, step-by-step fashion she will go to the prom with him.

The abstract sequential student usually does very well academically, though he or she may have problems with social skills. This student's intuitive and emotional skills are often weak.

This student likes to:

• read different kinds of books. This student usually has a library book to read when an assignment is finished or when he or she is bored with assigned schoolwork. Because of this preference for reading, this student generally has working knowledge in a variety of areas.

- listen to audio tapes, compact disks and lectures, see videos, films and slides, and work on the computer and other electronic learning tools. Generally, this is the student who is quite technologically oriented and may know more about the computer than the teacher does!

- help other students understand the subject matter or what they've read, and is usually willing to tutor a classmate or a group of younger students. On the other hand, this student is not very good at "small talk" when the topic is not defined.

- find THE answer to a problem, and is uncomfortable with multiple answers and possibilities. This student sees no reason to have brainstorming sessions that accept all answers and often doesn't see the purpose in "What would happen if . . ." questions. He or she may object to such a question asking, "But what actually did happen? Isn't that what is important?"

- look at things logically, even situations where a logical solution is not necessarily the best one or does not solve the problem.

The Concrete Random Learning Style

Thirteen year old Paul cheered and clapped when his history teacher said the class had a choice between doing either a written report or a project on the same topic covered in the thematic unit. As far as Paul was concerned, doing a project wasn't like doing 'real' school work at all. When the teacher asked the class to brainstorm project ideas, Paul's hand was constantly in the air. By the end of class, he was already thinking of how he could build a replica of a pioneer settlement using some twigs and branches he knew were in the woods behind his house. "I wish I could do this kind of stuff in all my classes," he thought to himself.

Schools traditionally have more trouble programming for students with random learning styles.

This student likes to:

- complete a product for a classroom assignment. Somehow this doesn't seem to be "work" like a written paper or a set of questions to be answered at the end of a chapter. This student will do an excellent job with a hands-on project, but unlike the concrete sequential student, may not turn it in on time.

- brainstorm creative ideas. This student is never worried about what the "right" answer is. Whether in a large or small group, this student will contribute many ideas in almost any brainstorming activity.

- take risks. Concrete random students will volunteer for anything, even if they do not know what it will involve, especially if it will get them out of class. Often, these students will get into trouble because of risk taking behavior!

- do things by trial and error. Don't give this student the directions and expect him to follow them! Instead, he will try different possibilities until he discovers a way of doing something that works best for him.

- solve problems alone. Group work is not these students' favorite. They would rather figure out the problem on their own, often by "fooling around" with concrete objects until something works out correctly.

- avoid IQ and achievement tests. These students normally do not do very well on multiple choice, true/false, or other types of objective tests. Because they can see multiple possibilities, even "wrong" answers may seem defensible to them. Essay and short answer tests, portfolio and alternative assessments, or class projects suit these students much better.

The Abstract Random Learning Style

Taneka, a 6th grader, has lots of friends and loves to talk. She enjoys her friends at school, and when she gets home from school the phone calls start. Her dad teases her, saying the phone is growing out of her ear! At school her talking bothers some of her teachers so they sit her in the front of the classroom, thinking this may keep her from talking. But most of the time she just turns around and talks anyway. Taneka likes to read and can tell you the titles of several favorite books. Usually she reads the first couple of chapters and then skims

over the rest, just getting the main ideas. She is likable, popular and has excellent leadership skills.

These are the students who are always talking.

This student likes to:

- listen to, learn from and respond to their classmates. They thrive on class discussions and wish that the teacher would structure class like a large discussion group all the time. Even when someone tries to "get the teacher off the subject" the abstract random learner learns from whatever he or she hears.

- work in groups. These are the students who benefit most from cooperative learning and other forms of group work. Often they will become the natural leaders in small groups and can make everyone feel included.

- read short reading assignments. They like to read, but find it hard to sit still long enough to read long books. Lots of shorter reading assignments suit them better.

- use emotions and intuition. Often these students come up with the right answer but can't tell you the logical steps of how they got it. Their thought processes are intuitive, not logical.

- have lots of things going on at once. They are the "jugglers" and think that the more things they do the better. They take on lots of new things but are not as good at following through over a long period of time.

Learning Styles

Teacher Reflection Page

List the names of one or more of your students and descriptive traits of each that fit each learning style.

Concrete Sequential:

Abstract Sequential:

Concrete Random:

Abstract Random:

Mixture of learning styles:

CLASSROOM ACTIVITIES

Which learning style(s) do you incorporate in your classroom?

1. List several activities you have done in your class in the past two or three weeks. Indicate the learning style(s) they are most suited for.

I. Activity:

Learning style(s):

II. Activity:

Learning style(s):

III. Activity:

Learning style(s):

IV. Activity:

Learning style(s):

2. Which style(s) do most of your classroom activities lend themselves to?

3. Which style(s) are most difficult for you to work with?

Using the Individual Student Lesson Plan format to plan units incorporating learning styles

After you have done the initial planning of your unit (see pages 17 and 19), decide which activities you want all of your students to do. As in the previous chapter, list these activities in the block in the center of the *Individual Student Lesson Plan* format labeled **Required Activities - Teacher's Choice.** List the products that will be turned in as a result of doing these activities and criteria for assessment in the two blocks on the right.

Now look at the remainder of the activities you listed. These will become your *Student Choice Activities.* Review the characteristics for each learning style. Decide which activities are appropriate for each learning style. Using a form similar to the one on the preceding page (*Classroom Activities*) may be helpful in making this determination. If you do not have enough activities for a particular learning style, look again at your unit objectives and questions. How could you design learning activities for each learning style that would meet the objectives and answer the unit questions? If you run out of ideas, have your students or a colleague brainstorm with you.

In planning *Inventors and Inventions*, one of the activities for the *Concrete Sequential* learner was to make a time line showing famous inventions. This activity would work well with the type of learner who likes to make charts and outlines. An activity appropriate for the *Abstract Sequential* learning style was to read a biography about a famous inventor and give an oral report to the class, because this is the type of student who loves to read and share this knowledge with other students. For the *Concrete Random* student, an appropriate activity would be to invent a 3-dimensional game about inventors. Remember this type of student likes doing "hands-on" projects. Finally, for the *Abstract Random* student, one of the activities was to choose an important invention and debate its merits with a classmate. This is the learning style that likes to learn from and respond to other students in the class.

On the next page is the *Individual Student Lesson Plan* with the student choices focusing on Learning Styles. A reproducible blank format with student choices by learning styles is on the following page. Use this to design your own units.

> "There will be no freedom without intelligence, And no real intelligence without heart."
>
> Luis Machado

INDIVIDUAL LESSON PLAN - LEARNING STYLES

Required Activities
Teacher's Choice

1. Read chapter on inventions in text. Outline or make a web of the information.
2. Define vocabulary words about inventions.
3. Listen to talk by guest speaker, a local inventor. Write a reaction paper.

Product/Performance
Required

1. Outline or web

2. Definitions

3. Reaction paper

Assessment
Required Activities

1. Understanding of main ideas

2. Accuracy

3. Supporting evidence/rationale for

Optional
Student-Parent
Cooperative Activity

Student Choices in
Ways to Learn
Concrete Sequential
_____

Concrete Random
_____

Abstract Sequential
_____

Abstract Random
_____

Product/Performance
Student Choice

Assessment
Student Choice

ACTIVITIES - STUDENT CHOICES

Concrete Sequential

1. Make a time line showing famous inventions.
2. Develop a chart comparing and contrasting the telephone, computer & television.
3. Draw a diagram of your invention for improving transportation to and from school.

Abstract Sequential

4. Read a biography about a famous inventor. Give an oral report to the class.
5. Write and illustrate a booklet showing how an invention works.
6. Make your list of the 10 most important inventions of the 20th century. Give reasons why these are the most important.

Concrete Random

7. Cut out a full-sized person from butcher paper. Make him a famous inventor. Write about him in the cut-out.
8. Invent a 3-D game about inventors.
9. Working in a small group, list 20 objects. Put them in random pairs. Then brainstorm all the possible inventions.

Abstract Random

10. Choose an important invention. Debate its merits with a classmate.
11. Develop a group skit showing what would have happened if TV was not invented.
12. Read about several inventors. Identify common characteristics and report to your class.

INDIVIDUAL LESSON PLAN - LEARNING STYLES

ACTIVITIES - STUDENT CHOICES

Required Activities Teacher's Choice	Product/Performance Required	Assessment Required Activities

Optional Student-Parent Cooperative Activity		
Student Choices in Ways to Learn	Product/Performance Student Choice	Assessment Student Choice
Concrete Sequential		
_____		
Concrete Random		
_____		
Abstract Sequential		
_____		
Abstract Random		
_____		

Concrete Sequential	Concrete Random

Abstract Sequential	Abstract Random

Structuring Student Choices

When giving students choices by learning style, it is important for them to experience working in more than one learning style. Everyone has a learning style preference; however in adult life we have to learn to function in all four. I have an Abstract Random learning style preference, yet I function in the Concrete Sequential style when I am catching a plane or scheduling workshops! No one has the luxury of remaining in just one style. For this reason, structure student choices so that each student has to work in at least two different styles. For example, you might have each student choose two activities from one style and one from a different style.

It is up to each teacher to decide how to structure the choices.

Remember, when you use the *Individual Lesson Plan* format you need to have some type of a timetable or schedule so that both the student and the teacher will know the due date for products and assignments.

Using the Individual Student Lesson Plan format in the mixed ability classroom

In a mixed ability classroom you can use these activities for everyone. You could have easier choices and more difficult choices. If you want all students to have the same choices, differentiate the quality, level and expectations for the products for gifted and other high ability students.

Students can also think of their own activities and write them on the chart in the appropriate places. These self-generated choices give you even greater flexibility to individualize for your students. Encourage your gifted students to think of specific higher level thinking activities they would like to do and write them on the chart. This also gives you an opportunity to help lower ability students choose activities which are not as difficult as the general student choice activities.

Reflections

* Learning styles indicate the ways in which people process information.

* Dr. Anthony Gregorc has identified four basic learning styles:

✓ concrete sequential
✓ abstract sequential
✓ concrete random
✓ abstract random

* Students need to learn how to identify their strong and weak styles and become adept at working in all styles.

* Use the *Individual Lesson Plan* format to plan student activities appropriate for each learning style.

---

[2] Griggs, S. & Dunn, R., "Selected Case Studies of Learning Style Preferences," Gifted Child Quarterly, Vol. 28, Number 3, p. 115-119, 1984.

Chapter 3

Learning Modalities

Questions to Consider

1. What do learning modalities indicate?

2. What are the four learning modalities?

3. How can learning modalities be included when planning curriculum, units, and lessons?

4. How can student choices be structured?

As I observed and worked with various groups of students over the past several years, it became clear that children learn in very different ways. A number of theories help educators understand these many differences in students. Some reflect individual differences in abilities or experiences, but educators can categorize and work with other differences by examining learning modalities. Like the learning styles discussed in the last chapter, the learning modalities that students use are another way to look at student learning.

Learning modalities indicate the modes, or means through which people acquire and work with information. Traditionally, educators have worked with three of these: Visual, Auditory/Verbal, and Kinesthetic. As the 21st century approaches and the Information Age dawns, we need to add a fourth modality: Technological. While technology incorporates elements of the other three, the mental processes, specific tools, and pieces of equipment students use when dealing with technology are significantly different from the other three to warrant a fourth category.

While most students learn to obtain and work with information in all four ways, each student usually has a modality strength. By observing your students, it is possible to identify their preferred modalities. It is not necessary for students to always acquire information in their preferred mode, but we should make an effort to allow them to choose their modality when possible.

Besides having strengths in one modality, some students may also have specific weaknesses in a particular modality. Often this is the case with identified students with learning disabilities, attention deficit disorder, or other learning difficulties or problems. By identifying areas of strength and weakness, you can more readily individualize the learning activities to best meet the requirements of students with special needs.

Gifted or high ability learners often have tremendous strengths in one modality but may be average or below average in the others. Contrary to popular opinion, gifted students are not usually gifted in every learning area or every modality. These students in particular may resist doing activities in which they will not excel,

> "Our chief need in life is someone who will make us do what we can."
>
> Ralph Waldo Emerson

though it is good to challenge them by having them do some things that do not come easily.

Consider both your students with special needs and your gifted students as you learn more about learning modalities in this chapter.

The Visual Modality

Benita is a good reader. She can recognize more words by sight than almost anyone else in her second grade class. When she is in the car or at the grocery store with her mom, she reads the road signs and food labels. Benita loves to draw and can usually visualize the finished product before she begins working on it. When her dad takes her to the playground on Saturdays, she calls out to him repeatedly, "Look at me! Look at me!" Playing isn't very much fun for her unless someone is watching what she is doing. When she wants to rearrange her room, she draws her plan on a piece of paper before moving the furniture around. Benita's learning modality is visual.

Students with *strengths* as visual learners:

- learn by seeing, watching demonstrations

- can recall the placement of words and pictures on a page

- are good with detail

- like descriptive reading and are affected by visual display and color

- recognize words by sight and people by face rather than name

- often remember whatever they have written down

- have a vivid imagination and think in pictures

- are deliberate problem solvers and plan solutions before acting

- use facial expressions that are a good indication of their emotions

- take in many visual images but may or may not concentrate on one image for a long period of time

Favorite Phrases: "Do you *see* what I mean?" "*Look* at me!"

Students with **weaknesses** as visual learners:

- often turn in papers that are not neatly done

- read numbers, mathematical signs or directions incorrectly

- do not do well on map activities

- get words or letters backwards

- leave out letters or words when writing

- don't notice when a room is redecorated

- have trouble copying from the board

- don't like to play Scrabble® or do crossword puzzles

To **increase visual skill**s in all students, use:

Products: charts, illustrations, film-strips, films, graphs, collages, murals, maps, time lines, flow charts, diagrams, posters

Activities: observe, copy, illustrate, design, imagine, color, draw, read

The Verbal (Written & Auditory) Modality

Laurel loves to talk. She talks a lot with her friends but she also talks to herself when she is trying to learn something, repeating the information over and over. Her favorite assignment in school this year was writing a poem about the environment. Her poem had so many 'plays on words' everyone thought it was hilarious. All of the lines rhymed, too. Laurel keeps a journal where she writes out all of her problems. She then talks about these problems with her mom and her best friend. She usually explains the problem to them and then asks, "Do you hear what I'm saying?" Laurel is a verbal learner.

Students with *strengths* as verbal learners:

- learn through verbal instructions from others or themselves

- like oral language

- enjoy dialogues, skits and debates

- have auditory word attack skills and learn words phonetically

- talk to themselves, repeating information verbally

- remember by verbal repetition but are distracted by sounds

- talk out problems, talk about pros and cons of a situation, and try out solutions verbally

- express emotion through changes in pitch, tone and volume of voice

- enjoy listening but are always ready to talk

- favor music, rap, poetry, rhyming words

- are not detail people; tend to be global thinkers

- memorize through verbal repetition

Favorite Phrases: "Do you *hear* what I'm saying?" "I'm just thinking *out loud.*"

Students with *weaknesses* as verbal learners:

- find it easier to show or demonstrate something than to tell about it

- know what they want to say but have a hard time finding the right words

- ask others to repeat what they've just said

- have difficulty listening in class

To *increase verbal, listening and auditory skills* in all students, use:

Products: oral reports, role plays, simulations, panel discussions, debates, lectures, skits, poetry, songs, audio tapes

Activities: interview, discuss, talk about, recite, debate, share, respond, explain, list, brainstorm, paraphrase, sing, memorize

The Kinesthetic Modality

Allen is a hands-on person. He loves to build models and has a big display of model airplanes and model cars in his room. He also enjoys watching adventure movies and likes to play basketball with his friends. In school his favorite subject is science because his teacher lets the students do lots of real experiments. Last week he actually was able to dissect a frog! Sometimes he gets in trouble at school because he wiggles around and is always out of his seat. He went to the principal's office a couple of times for fighting. Allen thinks school would be better if the teachers gave more assignments that dealt with 'real life'. When Allen finishes talking to someone on the phone he often says, "I'll be in touch with you again later." He functions best using the kinesthetic learning modality.

Students with *strengths* as kinesthetic learners:

• learn by direct involvement

• prefer action/adventure stories and videos

• remember what they have done more readily than what has been seen or read

• Believe hands-on experiences are important

• experiment with ideas to see how they will work in the real world

• touch, feel, manipulate, and play with objects

• show emotions physically by jumping, hugging, applauding, etc.

• communicate feelings through body language

• enjoy the performing arts and athletics

• like working with machinery and tools

Favorite Phrases: "How does that *grab* you?" or "Are you in *touch* with that?"

Students with **weaknesses** as kinesthetic learners:

• are not good at sports

• may be seen as clumsy and awkward

• are unskilled in working with their hands

• have trouble putting puzzles together

• would rather be a spectator than a participant

• may say they have "two left feet"

To **increase kinesthetic skills** in all students, use:

Products: diorama, puzzle, game, sculpture, model, puppet, scrapbook, mural, skit, pantomime, mobile

Activities: assemble, construct, invent, sort, put together, build, design, experiment, manipulate

The Technological Modality

From the time he was in first grade, Mark was the one teachers would call on to figure out any problem they were having with the computer. Even at a very young age, Mark seemed to have a natural affinity for technology. As computers got more powerful, Mark began writing his own programs, developing databases, designing computerized graphic images and learning to integrate audio and video into his school reports. Mark does much better work when he uses technological tools to accomplish it. His reports done on the word processor and complex math problems solved with the aid of a calculator are superior to the work he does without technological aids. Mark has many on-line friends from all over the world with whom he corresponds regularly via E-mail. Mark learns best through the technological learning modality.

Students with *strengths* as technological learners:

• would like to learn everything via the computer

• spend much of their spare time on the computer or playing video games

• know how to work with and use new software programs and new hardware

• enjoy using a video camera

• are mechanically oriented

• like integrated learning activities

• interact and communicate with others via E-mail and/or the Internet

• obtain information electronically

• understand how to integrate various technologies

Favorite Phrases: "Would you give me your *input* on that?" "I'm on *overload!*"

Students with **weaknesses** as technological learners:

• may be hesitant to even touch a computer

• are afraid that they will break the equipment if they try to use it

• don't like to experiment with new ways to do things technologically

• would rather write something by hand instead of using the word processor

• will let their partner do all of the hands-on work at the computer while they just sit and watch

To increase technological skills in all students, use:

Products: video or audio tape, computer generated report with graphics, original computer program, slides, photos, AutoCAD drawings

Activities: searching a database, generating graphs, developing electronic surveys, producing a word processing document, making a multimedia presentation

Using the Individual Student Lesson Plan format to plan units incorporating learning modalities

After you have done your initial planning of your unit decide which activities you want all of your students to do. List these activities in the block in the center of the *Individual Student Lesson Plan* format which is labeled **Required Activities - Teacher's Choice.** List the resulting products and criteria for evaluation in the two blocks on the right.

Now look at the remainder of the activities. Examine how students will gather information as they do each activity. If you have not listed very many activities in a particular modality, you can often make a small change so that the activity will fit a different modality than you had originally planned. These activities become the *Student Choice Activities.* Review the characteristics for each learning modality. Decide which activities would be appropriate for each. Using a form similar to the one on the following page may be helpful in doing this.

In planning my *Inventors and Inventions* unit, one activity I chose for the visual learner was to make a collage of 19th and 20th century inventions. This activity would work well for a visual learner who likes visual display and color and who thinks in pictures. An activity appropriate for the verbal learner is debating who the most important inventor of the 20th century is, because this is the type of student who likes dialogue, skits and debates. For the kinesthetic student, one appropriate activity would be to invent a 3-dimensional game about inventors. Remember this student likes to touch, feel and manipulate

objects. Finally, for the technological learner, one activity is to learn about an inventor or invention through using commercially developed software because this type of learner likes learning everything via the computer.

On the next page is the *Individual Student Lesson Plan* with the student choices focusing on Learning Modalities. A reproducible blank format with student choices by learning modalities is on the following page. Use this to design your own units.

Structuring Student Choices

Since students need to learn to work with information through all four modes, structure the student choices so that they must make choices in at least two different modalities. Students write their choices directly on the *Individual Student Lesson Plan,* as in the Learning Styles chapter.

Most students are anxious to try technological learning. However, your choices in this area may depend on the availability of technological equipment in your classroom or school. If this is a problem, brainstorm ways to get more equipment with your students and/or your principal.

INDIVIDUAL LESSON PLAN - LEARNING MODALITIES

ACTIVITIES - STUDENT CHOICES

Visual

1. Make a chart comparing/contrasting copyrights & patents. Write a paragraph about which one you think is most important & why.
2. Make a crossword puzzle of Leonardo DaVinci's inventions.
3. Make a collage of 19th century or 20th century inventions.

Verbal

7. Debate with a classmate: The most important invention of the 20th century is . . . because . . .
8. Using appropriate visual aids do an oral report about the car. Include your car of the future.
9. Write your list of the 10 most important inventions. Persuade the class that your list is correct.

Kinesthetic

4. Create a best friend robot and list 10 things you would like it to do.
5. Make a contraption from paper and explain how it works.
6. Invent a game and make a 3-D gameboard.

Technological

10. Produce a 5 minute musical video selling yourself as a robot.
11. Survey 25 people with home computers to find out what kind they have. Generate a chart or graph showing the survey results.
12. Use commercially developed software to find out about a specific invention and/or inventor.

Required Activities
Teacher's Choice

1. Read text about inventions & inventors. Answer text questions.
2. View video about major inventions of the 20th century. Make a mind map of important inventions.
3. Write a news story about one important inventor.

Product/Performance
Required

1. Answer to questions

2. Mind map

3. News story

Assessment
Required Activities

1. Accurate; complete

2. Main ideas recorded; appropriate details & facts

3. Organization; clarity of thought

Optional
Student-Parent
Cooperative Activity

Student Choices in
Ways to Learn

Visual
_____

Kinesthetic
_____

Verbal
_____

Technological
_____

Product/Performance
Student Choice

Assessment
Student Choice

INDIVIDUAL LESSON PLAN - LEARNING MODALITIES

ACTIVITIES - STUDENT CHOICES

Required Activities Teacher's Choice	**Product/Performance Required**	**Assessment Required Activities**

Optional Student-Parent Cooperative Activity

Student Choices in Ways to Learn Visual ___ Kinesthetic ___ Verbal ___ Technological ___	**Product/Performance Student Choice**	**Assessment Student Choice**

Visual	**Verbal**
Kinesthetic	**Technological**

©1997 Carolyn Coil and Pieces of Learning

Learning Modalities

Teacher Reflection Page

1. List the names of one or more of your students for each modality. Give examples of how they have used this modality to acquire and work with information.

   Visual:

   Verbal:

   Kinesthetic:

   Technological:

2. Which modality are you most comfortable using?

   Write some ways you have used this modality in your own learning.

3. Which modality is least comfortable for you? Why?

CLASSROOM ACTIVITIES

Which modalities do you incorporate in your classroom?

1. List several ways students generally gather information in your classroom. Indicate the modality each is most suited for.

Gather information in this way:

Learning modality:

Gather information in this way:

Learning modality:

Gather information in this way:

Learning modality:

Gather information in this way:

Learning modality:

---

2. What teaching activities or materials that you have not been using could you use to facilitate learning in each modality?

   Visual:

   Verbal:

   Kinesthetic:

   Technological:

Notes

Taxonomy of Educational Objectives

Taxonomies are classification schemes developed to delineate educational goals, objectives and outcomes. They provide a way for us to understand and develop questions, and because they are descriptions of types of behavior, they are observable.

When I was an undergraduate in the College of Education, one of the first educational ideas I learned was Bloom's Taxonomy. It has been part of my educational philosophy ever since then. I believe it continues to be a powerful tool for educators. It is extremely useful in providing guidance and structure as teachers plan objectives, learning activities and educational outcomes for their students.

Bloom's Taxonomy, also called the Taxonomy of Educational Objectives, is a frequently used model for developing higher level thinking skills. It is a process-oriented model that allows teachers to present ideas and concepts at many different levels. In this way, teachers can use it to help meet the needs of a variety of learners.

It is important to stimulate the brain at all levels; therefore expose all students to learning activities and experiences at different levels of the taxonomy. Often teachers choose simple objectives that require little student thinking. These tend to be at the lower levels of the taxonomy. When this happens, it is a cause for concern because we need to optimize the learning potential of all our students.

We often think of Bloom's Taxonomy as a linear model, but we can also view it as cyclical, with the evaluation level creating new information to be learned at the knowledge level. It can also be seen as a structure that facilitates a free flow of ideas and activities between the different levels. Teachers must be able to assess how much each student knows and comprehends about a given topic of study to know how much time each student needs to spend working at the lower levels of the taxonomy. Some students bring a large amount of knowledge to class with them and are ready to move to the higher levels very quickly.

The Taxonomy may be new to you. You may have learned about Bloom's Taxonomy years ago. You may have used it from time to time in planning lesson objectives or in examining performance levels for your students. Continue to use it or become reacquainted with it. This Taxonomy of Educational Objectives is an important tool for 21st century teachers.

The six levels of Bloom's Taxonomy and a brief descriptor of each are:

Knowledge - Acquiring/learning facts

Comprehension - Understanding the information on a basic level

Application - Using the information in a new context

Analysis - Examining the information in detail, one part at a time

Synthesis - Understanding the information in relation to the whole

Evaluation - Assessing the information based on agreed upon criteria

Level 1 - Knowledge

Ability to:

☐ bring to mind appropriate material and answers

☐ recall or recognize specific information

This level addresses the knowledge of specific facts and terminology, the ways students can deal with these specific facts, and categories or patterns of knowledge.

For example, in *Inventors & Inventions* at the knowledge level a student makes a poster of any three inventors and their inventions.

Representative Activities		Representative Products
Define	Describe	Lists
Label	Locate	Definitions
Recite	Select	Outlines
Memorize	Recognize	Map locations
Name	State	Answers to reproductive questions
Identify	Repeat	

Level 2 - Comprehension

Ability to:

☐ understand the information given or communicated

☐ make use of an idea in the same or similar situation

This level addresses the ways students interpret information.

For example, in *Inventors & Inventions* a student explains how the invention of his choice works.

Representative Activities

Restate	Paraphrase
Rewrite	Convert
Give examples	Illustrate
Summarize	Explain
Locate	Express

Representative Products

Essay	Diagram
Oral report	Drawing
Mural	Map with
	locations noted

Level 3 - Application

Ability to:

☐ use ideas, theories, methods, concepts, or principles in new situations

☐ use something in a different way

This level addresses the use of abstractions in particular situations.

For example, in *Inventors & Inventions* if a student has knowledge of which inventions have helped senior citizens lead safer lives, she could make a chart showing these inventions and explain to a group of senior citizens how to use them.

Representative Activities

Apply	Modify
Dramatize	Translate
Demonstrate	Construct

Representative Products

Diagram	Puzzle
Diorama	Model
Map	Mobile
Diary	Illustration
Collection	Journal

Level 4 - Analysis

Ability to:

☐ break down into smaller parts

☐ make something clearer by examining it closely

This level addresses the breaking of the whole into parts to distinguish elements, relationships or organizational principles.

For example, in *Inventors & Inventions* a student could develop a chart to compare and contrast similarities and differences among several different types of aircraft.

Representative Activities		**Representative Products**
Analyze	Classify	Graph
Distinguish	Subdivide	Questionnaire
Separate	Differentiate	Survey
Examine	Calculate	Chart
Compare/contrast		List of parts or classifications

Level 5 - Synthesis

Ability to:

☐ put together parts into a unified whole

☐ express original thoughts or make original products

This level addresses putting parts together in a new form such as in a new piece of writing or other form of communication, a new plan, or a new invention.

For example, in *Inventors & Inventions* a student might develop a new invention that combines both music and math.

Representative Activities		**Representative Products**	
Combine	Compose	Invention	News article
Design	Organize	Story	Poem
Invent	Develop	Play/skit	Original game
Plan	Create	Plan of action	

Level 6 - Evaluation

Ability to:

☐ judge the value of something according to specified criteria

☐ develop and apply standards and criteria

This level addresses making judgments based on logical evidence, external facts, and/or established criteria.

For example, in *Inventors & Inventions* a student might debate the question "What is the best form of transportation for the 21st century?"

Representative Activities		**Representative Products**	
Judge	Evaluate	Critique	Conclusion
Recommend	Summarize	Portfolio	
Debate	Criticize	Summary of group discussion	
		Review of a play, book, song, etc.	
		Evaluation form with criteria listed	

"A civilized society is one in which people have an appreciation of and a concern with the incredibly wide range of human needs, capacities and potentialities."

Dr. Alice Tay, Professor, University of Sydney

ASSESSING THINKING SKILLS USING BLOOM'S TAXONOMY

When forming objectives and outcomes for your students, learn to assess which levels of the taxonomy they use. This assessment form will help you analyze your learning activities by showing you in which levels of the taxonomy your students will be working when they do a particular activity.

Name of Activity _____

1. Knowledge

☐ Ability to recall or recognize specific information

☐ Ability to bring to mind appropriate answers

2. Comprehension

☐ Ability to understand what is being communicated

☐ Ability to make use of an idea in the same or similar situation

3. Application

☐ Ability to use ideas in new situations

☐ Ability to use something in a different way

4. Analysis

☐ Ability to break down into smaller parts

☐ Ability to make something clearer by examining it closely

5. Synthesis

☐ Ability to put together parts into a unified whole

☐ Ability to express original thoughts or make original products

6. Evaluation

☐ Ability to develop standards and criteria

☐ Ability to judge the value of something according to specified criteria

As with Learning Styles and Learning Modalities in the previous two chapters, one way to ensure exposure to all students of the various levels of the taxonomy is to use the *Individual Student Lesson Plan* format. In this case, Bloom's Taxonomy will provide the structure for the student choice learning activities.

When using Bloom's Taxonomy with the *Individual Student Lesson Plan* format, require that all students choose at least one or two items from the four higher levels of the taxonomy (application, analysis, synthesis and evaluation). This will ensure that every student is engaged in activities requiring higher level thinking skills. Some students will need to do very little at the lower levels of the taxonomy because they will already have the knowledge and comprehension about a given topic. Other students may not have the background knowledge and therefore would need to do more at this level. You can structure individual choices so as to meet the learning needs of each of your students.

The sample *Individual Student Lesson Plan* format on pages 54 and 55 show how activities from a unit on *Inventors & Inventions* can be organized using Bloom's Taxonomy. There is a blank *Individual Student Lesson Plan* format structured for Bloom's Taxonomy on pages 56 and 57. Use the blank format to create your own units of study.

Reflections

* Bloom's Taxonomy provides a structure for planning objectives, learning activities and educational outcomes for students.

* There are six levels of Bloom's Taxonomy: knowledge, comprehension, application, analysis, synthesis, and evaluation.

* Students can be exposed to learning activities in all levels of the taxonomy by using the *Individual Lesson Plan* format.

NOTES

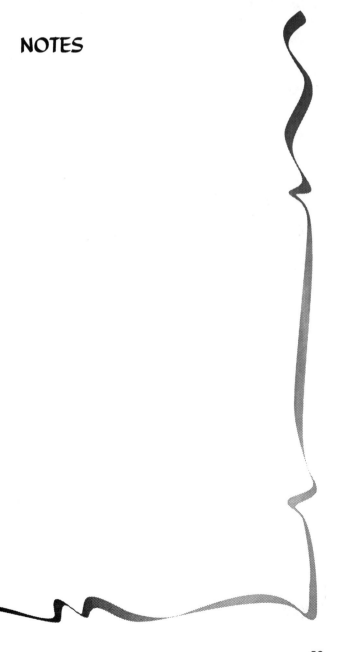

INDIVIDUAL LESSON PLAN - TAXONOMY OF LEARNING

Required Activities Teacher's Choice	Product/Performance Required	Assessment Required Activities
1. Read chapter in text that highlights significant inventions. Outline major ideas and details. 2. View video about important inventors of the 19th and 20th centuries. Write a summary. 3. Visit a local museum that features inventions from your state. Draw a diagram of one invention there.	1. Outline 2. Summary 3. Diagram	1. Choice of ideas and facts; accuracy 2. Clarity of thought; important details included 3. Appropriate visual; accuracy of information

Optional Student-Parent Cooperative Activity		
Student Choices in Ways to Learn Knowledge _____ Comprehension _____ Application _____ Analysis _____	Product/Performance Student Choice	Assessment Student Choice

©1997 Carolyn Coil and Pieces of Learning

ACTIVITIES - STUDENT CHOICES

Knowledge

1. Make a poster of any 3 inventors and their inventions.
2. Read a biography of a famous inventor. Present a short skit of his/her life & accomplishments.
3. Write to Disney World's Epcot Center to get information about inventions of tomorrow. Write a report about them.

Comprehension

4. In your own words explain how the invention of your choice works.
5. Write a mini book about the invention of the car. Include your car of the future.
6. Draw a cartoon that features an invention of the future.

Application

7. Make a chart of safety inventions for senior citizens. Share with groups of seniors.
8. Role play a typical day before electricity was invented.
9. Make a model of an invention that would do your homework automatically.

Analysis

10. Draw and label the parts of any 20th century invention. Explain the functions of each major part.
11. Develop a chart comparing and contrasting several different types of aircraft.
12. Make an oral report discussing problems in transition from the Industrial Age to the Information Age.

INDIVIDUAL LESSON PLAN - TAXONOMY OF LEARNING

ACTIVITIES - STUDENT CHOICES

Synthesis

13. Brainstorm all the functions you would like your personal robot to have. Then make a diagram of your robot showing how it would work.

14. Write a short story that illustrates changes in everyday life due to major inventions since 1900.

15. Invent a new invention that combines music and math.

Evaluation

16. Write a letter to Thomas Edison explaining why one of his inventions is so important.

17. Debate: Is it better to write on a computer or write with pencil and paper?

18. Decide on criteria for judging the best form of transportation.

Required Activities
Teacher's Choice

1. Read chapter in text that highlights significant inventions. Outline major ideas and details.

2. View video about important inventors of the 19th and 20th centuries. Write a summary

3. Visit a local museum that features inventions from your state. Draw a diagram of one invention there.

Product/Assessment
Required

1, Outline

2. Summary

3. Diagram

Assessment
Required Activities

1. Choice of ideas and facts; accuracy

2. Clarity of thought; important details included

3. Appropriate visual; accuracy of information

**Optional
Student-Parent
Cooperative Activity**

**Student Choices in
Ways to Learn**

Synthesis
_____
_____

Evaluation
_____
_____

Product/Performance
Student Choice

Assessment
Student Choice

INDIVIDUAL LESSON PLAN - TAXONOMY OBJECTIVES

Assessment Required Activities

Product/Performance Required

Required Activities Teacher's Choice

Assessment Student Choice

Product/Performance Student Choice

Optional Student-Parent Cooperative Activity

Student Choices in Ways to Learn

Knowledge

Comprehension

Application

Analysis

ACTIVITIES - STUDENT CHOICES

Comprehension

Knowledge

Analysis

Application

INDIVIDUAL LESSON PLAN - TAXONOMY OBJECTIVES

Required Activities Teacher's Choice	Product/Assessment Required	Assessment Required Activities

| Optional Student-Parent Cooperative Activity | | |

Student Choices in Ways to Learn	Product/Performance Student Choice	Assessment Student Choice

Synthesis ___ ___

Evaluation ___ ___

ACTIVITIES - STUDENT CHOICES

Evaluation

Synthesis

©1997 Carolyn Coil and Pieces of Learning

Chapter 5

Multiple Intelligences

Questions

1. What is intelligence?

2. Which intelligences are identified by Gardner's theory of Multiple Intelligences?

3. Can intelligence be developed and taught?

4. Do all students have multiple intelligences?

Mr. Briggs looked at Robyn, one of his most outstanding students. "She is so intelligent," he thought to himself. "She reads and writes beautifully and her work in math is always tops. I wish some of my other students were as intelligent as she is!"

In the above scenario, Mr. Briggs was describing the ways Robyn functioned in several tasks, activities and challenges she faces in school. To him, her responses in these areas define what an intelligent student is. Mr. Briggs, however, has a narrow view of intelligence, for his view focuses on verbal and mathematical tasks. He is not alone. Many of us who work in education have generally defined intelligence in a similar way.

But intellectual differences among people are much broader than this. To understand the concept of intelligence more fully, we need to examine the theory of Multiple Intelligences.

An Overview of Multiple Intelligences

Harvard University psychologist Howard Gardner developed his theory of Multiple Intelligences in the early 1980's. Saying educators and other experts had defined intelligence too narrowly, he stated that intelligence involves several different ways of solving problems and creating products. He demonstrated that each individual has a unique intelligence profile which shows relative strengths and weaknesses in all of the Multiple Intelligences. Each intelligence, he says, is modifiable and is sparked and activated by a variety of stimuli. Generally speaking, because of differences in culture and experience, in each individual some intelligences develop as dominant intelligences, others moderately, and some just slightly.

The Multiple Intelligences relate directly to whatever information or content is being dealt with. This means they are content based, rather than existing by themselves with no relationship to content. Handling different types of information leads to the development of different types of abilities. Intelligence is not a single fixed trait that can be assigned a single number for life! In fact, according to Gardner, we can develop and teach intelligence.

He came to this conclusion and developed his theory of Multiple Intelligences after studying children at the Boston University School of Medicine, the Veterans Administration Medical Center in Boston and at Harvard's Project Zero which sought to develop and enhance a variety of intelligences in young children. [3]

Intelligence and culture are interdependent. Different cultures put value on different types of intelligence. As a middle class white American, I have a highly developed verbal intelligence. My culture values this type of intelligence. Recently, however, I had the privilege of visiting an Aboriginal community at Daly River in the Northern Territory of Australia. As we drove from Darwin to Daly River, I began to sense the vastness and the silence of the Australian outback. The terrain changed subtly and seemed to stretch forever. I soon realized that visual and spatial intelligence (my weak area) would be much more valued in this environment than verbal ability. In this setting, I would not be considered very intelligent at all! This experience helped me understand the interrelatedness of one's culture and the development of one's intelligences.

Gardner suggests that each individual possesses seven different intelligences. Each person possesses a unique blend of these intelligences. In order to study and understand them, we can analyze each. But in "real life" people use them in combination with one another and not just one at a time.

Gardner believes that virtually everyone has the capacity to develop all seven of the Multiple Intelligences. The intelligences usually work together and interact with one another in complex ways. Most of the time when solving a problem, creating a product, or interacting with the environment, people use more than one intelligence. A student preparing for a debate, for example, will use Verbal/Linguistic intelligence but also Mathematical/Logical and Interpersonal intelligence.

Each intelligence exhibits itself in several ways. For example, a very quiet person who writes an excellent descriptive paragraph and a talkative person who tells a beautiful story but cannot write very well exhibit Verbal/Linguistic intelligence. Dancers or athletes who are performing and a craftsperson who is working very carefully with his hands exhibit Bodily/Kinesthetic intelligence. A mural with splashy brilliant colors and an architect's intricate drawings are both examples of Visual/Spatial intelligence.

The 3 Main Categories of Gardner's Multiple Intelligences

1. Language related	II. Object related	III. Personal related
Verbal/Linguistic	Logical/Mathematical	Intrapersonal
Musical/Rhythmic	Visual/Spatial	Interpersonal
	Bodily/Kinesthetic	

Naturalist

I. Language Related Intelligences

Verbal/Linguistic
Musical/Rhythmic

Described as "object free" intelligences, these two intelligences are reflected in the variety and forms of languages written and spoken all over the earth.

Verbal/Linguistic Intelligence

The ability to use language for a variety of purposes including to persuade, inform, communicate, solve problems, aid in memorization, entertain, and acquire new knowledge.

Jeremy, a first grader, knows he is the best reader in his class. He loves to read and began reading when he was three years old. His mom and dad read to him every night, and his dad always tells him a funny story before bedtime. His grandma gives him read-along books for every birthday, and he loves to listen to the stories as he turns the pages. He is learning to write sentences and paragraphs on a computer program at school. He is full of questions. Last week he wanted to know why the Smoky Mountains look like they are surrounded by smoke and why Kansas isn't near the ocean. He always has a new joke to tell his classmates and never forgets the punch line! Jeremy has a highly developed verbal/linguistic intelligence.

Characteristics:

- entails spoken and written language and its uses

- includes skill in speaking, writing, listening and reading

- relates to ability to learn new languages easily

- involves the capacity to use words effectively

- helps students produce and refine language in its many forms and formats

- enriched by a wealth of vocabulary

- embraces the ability to understand the function of language

Representative Products:

✓ Poem
✓ Speech
✓ Story
✓ Skit or play
✓ Newspaper article
✓ Oral report
✓ Word game
✓ Reaction paper

Representative Activities:

✓ Participating in a debate
✓ Writing a research paper
✓ Listening to a guest speaker
✓ Creating a new ending for a myth
✓ Acting in a dramatic reading
✓ Composing a story or poem

Representative Careers:

✓ Journalist
✓ Talk show host
✓ Speech writer
✓ Secretary
✓ Actor

Musical/Rhythmic Intelligence

The ability to communicate or understand emotions and ideas conveyed through music and the ability to compose and/or perform musically. Ideas, memories, factual information, emotions, moods, important historical or cultural events all can be incorporated into the musical/rhythmic intelligence.

Music has always been important to Ramon. When he was a little boy, special songs that he would hear at family gatherings seemed to bring all of them together. The radio is always blaring in his car and the CD player is always on in his room. Ramon is in 11th grade and has been in the school band since 7th grade. He practices his French horn every day and was excited to learn he has made first chair in the All-County band. Ramon has trouble in many of his academic subjects but finds he can memorize information if he puts it to music in his head. He has a highly developed musical/rhythmic intelligence.

Characteristics:

- is another form of language

- resides mostly in the right brain

- communicates without words

- involves sensitivity to sounds and a good sense of pitch

- is often highly emotional

- powerful in establishing and conveying mood

- involves the capacity to perceive, discriminate, transform and express musical forms

- includes both the intuitive understanding of music (such as playing an instrument "by ear") and a more formal, technical understanding (such as comes from the study of music theory)

- embraces rhythm, beat and harmony

- may assist in developing other intelligences

Representative Products:

✓ Song
✓ Audio musical advertisement
✓ Poem or rap
✓ Musical composition
✓ Musical performance
✓ Musical video

Representative Activities:

✓ Verbal recall in unison
✓ Singing songs tied to curriculum outcomes and objectives
✓ Choral reading
✓ Creating musical mnemonics
✓ Learning about, listening to and playing musical instruments

Representative Careers:

✓ Composer
✓ Ad writer
✓ Singer
✓ Instrumentalist in orchestra
✓ Band director
✓ Music teacher

II. Object Related Intelligences

Logical/Mathematical
Visual/Spatial Intelligence
Bodily/Kinesthetic

These three intelligences function along with the objects an individual works with when solving a problem or making a product.

Logical/Mathematical Intelligence

The ability to recognize and explore patterns, categories and relationships using objects or mathematical symbols in a logical, ordered, sequential way.

Carla is a third grader. She enjoys math, science and technology in school. She feels these subjects are much more logical than other subjects where the questions seem to have no right or wrong answers. Carla likes working with numbers. She has a large collection of sea shells displayed on a wide shelf in her home. Carla has classified all of them according to what type of shell they are. She also knows how the animals in each shell lived and how their shells protected them. Though she is considered 'smart' by her classmates, Carla has trouble making friends. When she plays a game, she knows all the rules and is dogmatic about sticking to them. The other students think she is 'bossy' because she does this so often. When she disagrees with others, she feels her view is totally right and theirs is totally wrong. She explains all the reasons she is correct without really listening to what anyone else is saying. Carla would not win any popularity contests in her class!

Characteristics:

- incorporates mathematical and scientific abilities

- oriented toward rules, rubrics and regulations

- characterized by both abstraction and exploration

- enjoys collecting and classifying things

- uses reasoning and logic to solve problems

- includes the capacity to use numbers effectively

- involves a sensitivity to logical patterns, statements and relationships

- can be very abstract

- entails knowing the practicalities of how things work

Representative Products:

✓ Graph
✓ Chart
✓ Time line
✓ Logic puzzle
✓ Venn diagram
✓ Solutions to math problems

Representative Activities:

✓ Comparing/contrasting
✓ Outlining
✓ Categorizing
✓ Finding patterns
✓ Observing/collecting data
✓ Doing mathematical operations

Representative Careers:

✓ Engineer
✓ Statistician
✓ Computer programmer
✓ Scientist
✓ Accountant
✓ Marine biologist
✓ Environmental regulator

Visual/Spatial Intelligence

The ability to perceive, create and change visual objects mentally; create and interpret visual arts; orient oneself using maps, blueprints or other visuals; navigate within an environment, specific space, or location.

When twelve year old Jennifer walks into a room, she immediately wants to re-decorate it! She can picture the way it would look with a new color of paint, new wallpaper and a new carpet on the floor. Jennifer wears clothes with colors and patterns most people would not think to put together, but she has an 'eye' for creating new visual images that work. Jennifer's friends say she is very creative and artistic. She loves to draw and spends much time sketching and doodling, even when she should be doing something else. Her favorite class is art, and she loves doing projects in other classes where she can use her artistic abilities. Jennifer hopes to be an architect, clothing designer or interior decorator when she grows up.

Characteristics:

• involves ability to represent spatial information graphically

• uses ability to respond to and recreate the visual world and to see things in a way others would not

• includes sensitivity to color, line, shape, form, space, and the relationships that exist between these elements

• incorporates the capacity to both visualize and to physically orient oneself spatially

• entails understanding of the relationship of parts to the whole object

• related to ability to read and interpret maps, charts and graphs

• requires a keen eye for visual detail

Representative Products:

✓ Painting
✓ Model
✓ Collage
✓ Mural
✓ Map
✓ Cartoon/comic strip
✓ Video
✓ Photo
✓ Drawing
✓ Origami
✓ Charts/graphs
✓ Web/mind map
✓ Computer graphics
✓ Diorama

Representative Activities:

✓ Using visual/graphic organizers
✓ Making bulletin boards, posters, mobiles
✓ Learning through color coding, colorful overheads, slides and videos
✓ Working with computer graphics programs
✓ Observing and participating in demonstrations
✓ Dissecting and/or taking things apart

Representative Careers:

✓ Cartographer
✓ Artist
✓ Photographer
✓ Graphic designer
✓ Clothing designer
✓ Food stylist
✓ Interior decorator
✓ Display artist

Bodily/Kinesthetic Intelligence

The ability to use both mind and body in the display of motor skills and the performance of physical tasks and to easily manipulate objects within one's environment.

Tony is a ninth grader who is already considered a top player on the high school football team. He has always loved sports and has played football ever since he can remember. Tony keeps his body in good shape, working out at least two hours a day during the off season. Catching a pass, running with the ball and eluding the other team's players comes as second nature to him. When he's not on the field, he often sees the game in his mind and mentally runs through the plays. Tony struggles academically and sometimes wishes reading, writing and math would come as easy for him as playing football does.

Characteristics:

• incorporates control of bodily motions and the ability to manipulate and interact with objects skillfully

• involves expertise in using one's whole body to express ideas and feelings

• related to a good sense of balance and grace in movement

• entails solving problems by "doing"

• requires good eye-hand coordination

• includes ability to use one's hands to produce or transform things

• uses physical skills such as coordination, balance, strength, speed and dexterity

Representative Products:

✓ Sports performance
✓ Dance
✓ Item made by hand
✓ Skit/pantomime
✓ Oral presentations
✓ Carving/sculpture
✓ Poster
✓ 3 dimensional game
✓ Design
✓ Model
✓ Demonstration
✓ Constructions

Representative Activities:

✓ Role playing
✓ Creative movement
✓ Outdoor education
✓ Math manipulatives
✓ Creating/inventing something
✓ Simulations
✓ Lab experiments
✓ Constructing models
✓ Cooperative learning
✓ Field trips
✓ Learning centers
✓ Active learning

Representative Careers:

✓ Sports medicine
✓ Chiropractor
✓ Building construction
✓ Lab technician
✓ Dental hygienist

✓ Plumber
✓ Massage therapist
✓ Carpenter
✓ Repair person

III. Personal Intelligences

Intrapersonal Interpersonal

Reflects the personal vision each individual has of himself and his relationships with others, and knowledge of cultural norms and social skills in a given society or group.

Intrapersonal Intelligence

The ability to have an awareness of, know, and understand one's own hopes, dreams, goals, aspirations, emotions, thoughts, ideas and convictions. It includes recognition of both strengths and weaknesses and the ability to reflect on one's own life.

Trent is quiet and shy, but when he believes in something he will express his feelings strongly. His classmates like Trent because they always know where they stand with him. His best friend describes Trent by saying, "When he says something, you know he's really thought it through." Trent is self confident and likes the quote from Aristotle, 'Know thyself.' He knows both his strengths and weaknesses and works hard to improve in his weak areas. He is a goal setter and when he accomplishes one goal he begins working on another. He daydreams quite a bit, thinking of all the possibilities of life. Trent writes down some of his deepest thoughts in a personal poetry journal but doesn't let anyone read it. He would like to be a psychologist when he grows up and has begun to research what types of jobs there might be in that field.

Characteristics:

• focuses inward in reflecting upon, analyzing and understanding one's own feelings and desires

• includes the ability to draw on emotions to direct one's own behavior

• involves the capacity for self-discipline and self-understanding

• uses both strengths and limitations in goal setting, motivation, and planning

• recognizes one's own needs and expectations

• learns from successes and failures

• does not require external approval for actions or convictions

• has strong preferences and is not easily swayed by others

Representative Products:

✓ Autobiography
✓ Journal or diary
✓ Reflective poetry
✓ Interest inventory
✓ Culture poster
✓ Assessments of strengths/weaknesses

Representative Activities:

✓ Independent study
✓ Journal/poetry writing
✓ Personal problem solving
✓ Boundary breakers

Representative Careers:

✓ Psychologist
✓ Ministry
✓ Guidance counselor
✓ Psychiatrist

Interpersonal Intelligence

The ability to sense the moods, feelings and needs of others, build relationships, display leadership skills, and work collaboratively and effectively as a member of a team.

Kris and Kim are twins who are in the eighth grade. Everyone likes them, and they seem to have a natural ability to get along with everyone—no matter what their race or ethnic group, and no matter what clique they belong to. The teachers are uniformly positive in their praise of Kris and Kim. They are hard workers in school and do particularly well in group discussions and cooperative learning situations. The girls seem to work better when they can talk about their ideas with others. They are not necessarily the smartest students in the eighth grade, but they are two of the easiest to work with. The twins are leaders in the Conflict Mediation Team at school and have prevented many fights and interpersonal conflicts throughout the school year.

Characteristics:

- focuses outward toward others and one's environment

- requires being able to do one's part for the good of the group

- involves the ability to understand and empathize with others

- includes sensitivity to both verbal and nonverbal cues and the ability to respond appropriately to them

- characterized by the ability to perceive the moods, intentions, feelings and motivations of others

- asks for, listens to and considers advice and opinions of others when making a decision

- oriented toward sharing with others

Representative Products:

✓ Dialogues
✓ Cooperative group project
✓ Solutions to problems done in a group
✓ Group symbols/logos
✓ Persuasive speech
✓ Story written by a group
✓ Debate
✓ Project to help people in the community

Representative Activities:

✓ Group work
✓ Brainstorming
✓ E-mailing other people
✓ "Talking" on the Internet
✓ Pinwheel brainstorming
✓ Games for two or more
✓ Group problem solving
✓ Developing teamwork skills
✓ Peer counseling
✓ Peer teaching/mentoring
✓ Class meeting
✓ Class discussion

Representative Careers:

✓ Salesperson
✓ Public relations
✓ Politician
✓ Teacher
✓ Mediator
✓ Lawyer

Multiple Intelligences
Student Characteristics

Name at least one of your students with specific strengths in each of the Multiple Intelligences listed below. Include characteristics or behaviors.

Intelligence	Student(s)	Characteristics/Behaviors
Verbal/ Linguistic		
Musical/ Rhythmic		
Logical/ Mathematical		
Visual/ Spatial		
Bodily/ Kinesthetic		
Intrapersonal		
Interpersonal		

Students' Strengths and Weaknesses in the Multiple Intelligences

It is helpful to be aware of our students' strengths and weaknesses in the Multiple Intelligences. Children usually have strengths in several areas, not just one. Teachers using the Multiple Intelligences can identify strengths and then use these strengths to build up weak areas.

Sometimes students misbehave because of a weakness in one of the Multiple Intelligences. For example, the student who is always in physical fights with others may have a weakness in Interpersonal intelligence. At the same time, he may be showing his strength in the Bodily/Kinesthetic intelligence, though in a very inappropriate way!

Thomas Armstrong suggests that one good way to identify students' most highly developed intelligences is to observe how they misbehave in class! The child who is always talking when he should not be most likely has highly developed Verbal/Linguistic and Interpersonal intelligences. The child who is always doodling on a piece of paper instead of doing problems in math is probably strong in the Visual/ Spatial intelligence. The student who always seems to have something in his hands to fiddle around with is probably strong in Bodily/Kinesthetic abilities. Although these students are misbehaving in some way, they are all demonstrating their areas of strength.

For too long educators and parents have labeled some children "smart" or "bright" while calling others "dumb" or "stupid" or "slow learners." When adults use these labels, often what may be happening is that the child may be functioning in an intelligence that is unfamiliar or uncomfortable to the teacher or the parent.

Think about typical types of misbehavior in your classroom. Use the *Teacher Reflection Page* on the next page to identify these and the intelligences they may indicate. I have given you some sample misbehavior to help you get started.

> "Using Multiple Intelligence theory can greatly affect students' behaviors in the classroom simply by creating an environment in which teachers recognize and attend to individual needs throughout the school day. Students are less likely to be confused, frustrated or stressed out in such an environment."
>
> Thomas Armstrong
> "Multiple Intelligences in the Classroom"

Common Misbehavior in Your Classroom: Which Intelligences Might They Indicate?

Teacher Reflection Page

Type of Misbehavior	Intelligence(s) Indicated	Positive uses of this Intelligence
Always talking	Verbal/Linguistic Interpersonal	Oral report Group discussion
Doodling/drawing	Visual/Spatial	Charts & graphs Posters
Fiddling with objects	Bodily/Kinesthetic	Math manipulatives Constructing a project

_____

_____

_____

_____

_____

_____

_____

_____

_____

Using Multiple Intelligences in Curriculum Planning

The Multiple Intelligence theory is a good model for assessing teacher strengths and weaknesses. Traditionally schools have concentrated heavily on the Verbal/Linguistic and the Mathematical/Logical intelligences. However, as we approach the 21st century with a more diverse student population, more diverse needs in the workplace, and more skills necessary for an educated citizenry, we need to use all seven intelligences as tools for curriculum planning as we design learning activities for students.

Think about which of the Multiple Intelligences you use most often in your teaching and which you try to avoid. Do you use seven different ways of teaching or do you concentrate on just one or two? Do you try to include all seven but just one at a time? Many activities incorporate more than one intelligence. Check yourself with the sample techniques and strategies below. When you plan classroom activities, which of these do you include?

☐ Brainstorming
(Verbal/Linguistic and Interpersonal)

☐ Word games with body movement
(Verbal/Linguistic and Bodily/Kinesthetic)

☐ Classifying using Venn Diagrams
(Mathematical/Logical and Visual/Spatial)

☐ 3 dimensional models/constructions
(Visual/Spatial and Bodily/Kinesthetic)

☐ Rap and poetry
(Verbal/Linguistic, Musical/Rhythmic and Intrapersonal)

☐ Journals
(Verbal/Linguistic and Intrapersonal)

☐ Cooperative learning
(Bodily/Kinesthetic and Interpersonal)

☐ Dissecting/taking things apart
(Visual/Spatial and Bodily/Kinesthetic)

☐ Graphs and charts
(Mathematical/Logical and Visual/Spatial)

☐ Hands-on learning
(Visual/Spatial and Bodily/Kinesthetic)

☐ Creative daydreaming
(Visual/Spatial and Intrapersonal)

☐ Math concepts set to music
(Mathematical/Logical and Musical/Rhythmic)

This checklist of sample classroom activities should focus your thinking on how you are using and can use Multiple Intelligences in your classroom. It is essential that teachers consider and include a variety of these intelligences when planning lessons. To plan appropriate classroom activities for students with various Learning Modalities and Learning Styles (as we discussed in previous chapters) you must use the Multiple Intelligences. The *Teacher Reflection Page* and Multiple Intelligences Lesson Planning Form on pages 71 and 72 will help you consider how to best incorporate Multiple Intelligence theory into your classroom planning.

Multiple Intelligences

Teacher Reflection Page

1. List several activities you have done in your class in the past two or three weeks. Indicate the Multiple Intelligence(s) they are most suited for.

   Activity:

   Multiple Intelligence(s):

   Activity:

   Multiple Intelligence(s):

   Activity:

   Multiple Intelligence(s):

   Activity:

   Multiple Intelligence(s):

   Activity:

   Multiple Intelligence(s):

2. Which of the intelligences do most of your classroom activities focus on?

3. Which intelligences are most difficult for you to work with?

4. Use the form on the next page to plan an activity for each of the multiple intelligences that you could use with your next unit of study.

Multiple Intelligences Lesson Planning Form

Unit of Study: _____

Intelligence   Student Activity or Activities

☐ **Verbal/Linguistic:** _____

_____

_____

☐ **Musical/Rhythmic:** _____

_____

_____

☐ **Logical/Mathematical:** _____

_____

_____

☐ **Visual/Spatial:** _____

_____

_____

☐ **Bodily/Kinesthetic:** _____

_____

_____

☐ **Intrapersonal:** _____

_____

_____

☐ **Interpersonal:** _____

_____

_____

Reflections

* Intelligence can be defined in many different ways.

* Howard Gardner's Theory of Multiple Intelligences states there are at least seven types of Intelligence:

Verbal/linguistic

Musical/rhythmic

Logical/mathematical

Visual/spatial

Bodily/kinesthetic

Intrapersonal

Interpersonal

* Intelligence can be developed and taught. It is not one fixed number assigned in early childhood and kept for life.

* All students have strengths and weaknesses in the Multiple Intelligences.

[3] Keynote by Dr. Howard Gardner, Edyth Bush Symposium On Intelligence: Theory into Practice, January 11,1992, Tampa, Florida.

Assessment

I have worked with teachers and students in many school districts on test taking skills. Without exception, I have found dedicated, worried teachers and administrators who are concerned that their students won't do well (or haven't done well in the past) on the high stakes required standardized tests. These educators want to do everything possible to prepare their students in test taking skills and ensure that their students will be successful.

While there are several strategies we can use to develop test taking skills, I wonder about this large national concern regarding standardized test scores. There are some basic questions we need to ask ourselves about testing, assessment and evaluation. What is the real purpose of assessment? What sorts of evaluative information do we need about each student? How often should we assess students and report on their progress? In this chapter, we will consider these issues.

Standardized Tests: Importance and Pitfalls

Standardized testing is an important and widely recognized instrument for measuring student learning across the United States. It is seen as a means of addressing accountability and determining educational progress, and is considered so important because it has the power to change children's lives. As a society, we constantly compare children to one another via their test scores. Tests can determine which classes students will take, which schools they will attend, and what their academic potential is. They have a powerful influence on what goes on in the classroom. In many school districts, passing the standardized test is the ticket to promotion to the next grade level or to graduation itself.

Tests influence school goals, dominate instruction, and reflect teacher performance. In some programs, they are the deciding factor in establishing levels of program funding. Newspapers print test scores on the front page, comparing one school or school district with another. Realtors use them to recommend the best school or school district to live in. And they are one means through which university researchers identify effective schools and through which high school students gain admittance to higher education.

Given all of this, there is generally a wide gap between the lessons taught in school and the content of standardized tests. These tests are usually disconnected from the essential purposes and objectives of the curriculum, and when much time is spent on them, the possibilities for student learning in other areas become more limited.

In many schools, students have less time to develop strengths and interest areas because they are spending more and more time in drill and practice sessions for multiple-choice exams. As a result, getting the right answer has become the goal and convergent thinking the norm. Divergent thinking and creativity have been de-emphasized. Many tests minimize the ambiguity of tasks and answers; thus, test items tend to be deliberately simplified. Unfortunately, students' abilities to use knowledge critically or creatively are not assessed well in this process. In fact, "thinking" test takers often defeat themselves by looking too far below the surface of the questions, and end up scoring lower than they should.

Testing is the mode of assessment that is weakest in showing students' true strengths and capacities. Standardized tests do not provide us with much information about student learning. They do provide standardized data which educators can use to assess student progress from one year to the next. They also provide a means of national, state, and schoolwide comparisons in a country where education is so fragmented and localized. Additionally, they sample content effectively and can be scored quickly.

Because these tests have taken on such importance, teaching to the test has become more and more common. The result has been rising test scores without comparable demonstrations that the students are really learning significantly.

As we enter the 21st century, the importance of standardized testing will probably not diminish. For the future, it will be with us in one form or another. Skills in studying for and taking tests are essential for success in today's schools. Therefore, you must include these skills in the repertoire of skills you teach your students. Here are some suggestions:

- ☐ Share every test taking tip you know.

- ☐ Demystify tests for your students. Many students think test items come out of thin air. Show them how tests are constructed.

- ☐ Encourage your students to study for tests together or to study with their parents.

- ☐ Find out ways to lessen test anxiety for your students.

- ☐ Share your own strategies and "tricks of the trade" for test taking and test making.

- ☐ Have your students write their own tests and quizzes for classroom tests.

For more information on *Test Taking Skills*, including *Dealing with Test Anxiety, Memorization Techniques, Time Management, Making Correct Choices on Multiple Choice Tests,* and *Taking Essay Exams,* see **Motivating Underachievers: 172 Strategies for Success** and **Becoming an Achiever: A Student Guide** by Carolyn Coil, Pieces of Learning.

Keep in mind — Student assessment is much more than test taking!

Performance Assessment vs Assessment through Testing

Two philosophies of student assessment seem to coexist in American education as we enter the 21st century. Many educators advocate assessing student performance in context through various means of authentic assessment, strategies where students show what they know through products, performances or portfolios of their work. Many others stakeholders in the educational system feel that the best way to see what students have learned is to use large-scale generic tests. This kind of testing assumes that knowledge can be decomposed into small elements and that it can always be known out of context. The tension between these two beliefs about assessment and education can be felt in almost every school district in our country.

Many tests given to students provide a means for us to judge superficial content knowledge, but they tend to bear little relationship to the real practice of the subject. Right and wrong multiple choice tests are not very much like real life. They are inherently restricted to unambiguous items, whereas real life is filled with ambiguity. In real life we use our intellect, knowledge and skills in a given situation to solve a certain problem. There is a difference between taking a test where there is one right answer and completing a product or performance where a variety of knowledge and skills are used to respond to the particular task at hand. A product or performance is done in context and involves constant judgment in adapting knowledge.

In a testing situation, students are handicapped in their access to factual knowledge or sources of information as compared to real life. When students take a test, they generally are not allowed access to their notes, reference materials or human resources. All they can use are the facts they have managed to memorize. A standardized test therefore cannot show how students sift through all the facts, synthesize information or use knowledge to good effect. Certainly in real life this is never the case. I would hate to be writing this book, for instance, without access to notes, reference materials and a host of human resources! Why not allow students to bring their notes to a test if our aim is to see what they understand, not just what they have managed to memorize for the short term?

Assessment is the process of collecting and organizing information so that it can be judged or evaluated. It should include all the processes we use for gathering information about student learning to meet a variety of evaluation needs. Assessment data becomes an indicator of what and how students are learning. It should include a variety of strategies and procedures. We assess students through tests, but they are only one part of the assessment process. In the next portion of this chapter, we will look more closely at alternative assessment methods.

> "An intelligence is a biological and psychological potential and is capable of being realized to a greater or lesser extent as a consequence of the experiential, cultural, and motivational factors that affect a person."
>
> Howard Gardner

From "Reflections on Multiple Intelligence: Myths and Messages," Phi Delta Kappan, Vol. 77, Number 3, Nov. 1995.

Assessment

Teacher Reflection Page

Think about some of the issues regarding assessment which are paramount in your own school and school district. Reflect on the questions below with at least one of your colleagues.

1. How much time do you spend in preparing your students for standardized tests?

2. What connections do you see (if any) between the content covered on the tests and the curriculum you are teaching?

3. How can you help demystify the testing process for your students?

4. In which test taking skills are your students strong? What are their weaknesses? How can you help them work on these?

5. How open are you to using various alternative methods of assessment? Does the school administration support alternative assessment? Do the parents understand it?

6. What problems do you see in using alternative assessment? What advantages do you feel alternative assessment has over traditional methods of assessing students?

Authentic Assessment Methods: Alternatives to Tests

Some terms you may hear when assessment is discussed include "authentic," "alternative," and "performance" assessments. These terms are used more or less interchangeably to indicate types of assessment strategies which go beyond paper and pencil testing and which are linked more directly to the purposes and meaning of what is taught rather than on testing specific skills and subskills. They usually get closer to assessing what students are actually learning because they are rooted in student performance on various learning tasks.

Performance assessment includes projects, products or performances which are used to exhibit those things students have learned. Performance based assessments can be linked to student learning as follows:

• Students know they have learned something when they can explain their work and ideas to others or when they can successfully teach others difficult concepts or content.

• Students know they have learned something when they are able to apply the knowledge to new problems or situations.

• Students know they have learned something when they create projects that actually work.

Alternative assessment methods go hand-in-hand with the various curriculum and educational reforms in schools. There is a close connection between alternative assessments and classroom instruction.

75% of students who are involved in performance assessment tasks say they prefer them over more traditional forms of assessment such as tests and written reports. They feel performance assessments allow people to see what they are really capable of doing and help them think for themselves. They also state that such assessments require more maturity, ownership and self motivation on the part of the student and a great deal more work.[4]

Alternative assessment includes activities such as the following:

• Portfolios of student work and performance-based tasks

• Student logs, rating scales and checklists

• Classroom discussions for sharing student work, examining strategies for improving it and evaluating it in terms of what they like and dislike

• Peer response sessions and interviews where students make thoughtful responses about their work

• Formal reflections where students review their past work and reflect on their growth and learning over time. These serve as evidence of evolving strengths and weaknesses

Linking Assessment with Instruction

Alternative forms of assessment differ quite dramatically from paper-pencil tests. One of the goals of assessment is to enhance the teaching and learning process. Assessment and evaluation should be contextualized, that is, rooted in instructional programs, not apart from them. When assessment measures are specific and relate directly to school and classroom based instruction, students tend to be more successful and assessment outcomes tend to be higher.

Performance assessments serve as a connection between instruction and assessment. They provide a means through which instruction and assessment can be woven together. Presentations, projects and performance samples are three types of performance assessment which link easily with instruction. These usually have a meaningful context in which knowledge is used in a setting important to the student. In this way, such assessment tasks encourage higher level thinking processes where knowledge and skills are applied in a new situation.

Many of the projects and products used in the *Individual Student Lesson Plan* format in this book are good examples of performance assessment tasks. They are tied directly to classroom instruction yet can also be used for assessment. Designing performance assessment tasks such as these will help you to focus on what you expect students to know and what outcomes and competencies you are teaching toward. Performance assessments highlight student work and should promote high-quality performance. This approach usually aligns assessment and instruction because there is an effort to match assessment to student work.

Designing Performance Assessment Tasks

Picture a group of students in front of a panel of teachers, parents and experts presenting and discussing their portfolios and demonstrating their projects which show they have met the school's standards and learning outcomes in a particular area. The criteria for assessing and evaluating their work has been established and is understood by all involved. Each student's work will be self-assessed as well as involved in peer assessment, teacher assessment and feedback from an outside expert. Such students are engaged in the final activity of an authentic performance assessment task.

In order to design performance assessment tasks, teachers must first decide what their students should be able to know and do. Then they need to decide what learning activities students must experience in order for them to demonstrate this knowledge in some way. To accomplish this, teachers must think through the curriculum content to establish learning outcomes or objectives, design performance activities which will allow students to demonstrate their achievement of these outcomes, and specify criteria by which they will be evaluated.

Alternative assessment is much more time consuming than traditional assessment! However, the results can be used as tools which show us much more about student learning than more traditional assessments do. Let's examine some of the more common types of alternative assessment in more detail.

Portfolios

Portfolios are a representative collection of students' work which has been done over a period of time. They are a means of documenting student learning and showing persons outside of the classroom what has been accomplished in school. Portfolios provide a way to show individual student growth and achievement by exhibiting a range of work.

Portfolios offer the opportunity to observe students in a broader context than traditional assessment can. In addition to assessing products and performances, portfolios can also be used to assess process skills. For example, depending upon what is chosen for the portfolio, it can show the amount of risk taking that was done by the student in choosing a product or activity. The student who always chooses the easiest or least challenging project may need to reflect on how to be more of a risk taker. Portfolios can also show leadership characteristics, how well a student works with others, and time management and organizational skills. Criteria reflecting growth in these skills can be part of a student log, checklist, or portfolio assessment form.

Portfolios have been called the "intersection of instruction and assessment" because they provide a means through which instruction and assessment can be woven together. Portfolios require students to collect and reflect upon examples of their own work and make choices about which is representative of their knowledge and learning. In this way, they encourage students to become participants in their own assessment.

Things to Consider Using Portfolios

Before using portfolios with your students, it is best to discuss these issues and concerns with them:

• What will it look like?

• How will it be structured?

• What should go in it?

• What will best show progress toward learning goals?

• Will it show only the best work (showcase portfolio) or will it show work which documents improvement?

• How and when will work samples be selected for the portfolio?

• What standards will be used to evaluate the portfolio?

• How much will the portfolio be counted in the final assessment, grade or evaluation of the work done in the class?

• How will evaluation criteria reflect standards of excellence, effort, and growth?

Observations, Checklists and Rating Scales

Observations, checklists and rating scales are often built upon the formal and informal assessment practices teachers already use. Teachers who work with students on a daily basis intuitively know their students, can understand their questions and can address their growth as learners. These assessment measures provide a way to document student growth and record information that teachers note on a regular basis about a child. This also includes notes on interests, behavior, thinking, and relationships,

Observational records come in various shapes, types and sizes. Some examples are rating forms, narrative descriptions, checklists, logs, and anecdotes. They help students and teachers recognize strengths and weaknesses. They can then mutually develop strategies to improve. Formal observations help teachers find out if a child has learned certain things and often indicate things about students they would otherwise have missed.

Informal folders and inventories such as checklists provide necessary documentation and give teachers a way to keep records about students' work. They facilitate a way to keep track of student activities and what each student has been involved in. While the best formats are teacher produced, some reproducible checklists used to identify students' affective and academic strengths and weaknesses can be found on the next four pages. Two are appropriate for K-3 students and two for grades 4 and above.

Academic Characteristics of Students
Who Are Becoming Achievers...

1. Rate your strengths and weaknesses in these areas.
2. Check S for each of your strengths.
3. Then count the number of S's.
4. Check W for weaknesses, but do not check more W's than S's.
5. You may leave some items blank!

S   W

_____ _____   I love reading.

_____ _____   I do well in at least one part of my schoolwork.

_____ _____   I can do math well.

_____ _____   I always have my school supplies.

_____ _____   I come to school on time.

_____ _____   I listen to the teacher.

_____ _____   I ask my teacher for help.

_____ _____   School is important to me.

_____ _____   I like art and music.

_____ _____   I like to work with my hands.

Personal Characteristics of Students Who Are Becoming Achievers...

1. Rate your strengths and weaknesses in these areas.
2. Check S for each of your strengths.
3. Then count the number of S's.
4. Check W for weaknesses, but do not check more W's than S's.
5. You may leave some items blank!

S   W

_____ _____   I like myself.

_____ _____   I say, "I can do it!"

_____ _____   I like school.

_____ _____   I love my teacher.

_____ _____   I have friends.

_____ _____   I follow the rules.

_____ _____   I think I learn a lot in school.

_____ _____   I listen to the teacher.

_____ _____   I share with others.

_____ _____   I treat other people kindly.

_____ _____   I have a special interest area.

Academic Characteristics of Students Who Are Becoming Achievers..

Rate your strengths and weaknesses in these areas. Check S for each of your strengths. Then count the number of S's. Check W for weaknesses, but do not check more W's than S's. You may leave some items blank!

S W

___ ___ I feel that at least one subject/topic/class in school is interesting
___ ___ and worthwhile.

___ ___ I have good organizational and time management skills.

___ ___ I am able to comprehend reading assignments in the subjects I take.

___ ___ I find it easy to memorize unfamiliar information.

___ ___ I like to have high quality in my schoolwork.

___ ___ I keep working and don't give up on subjects that don't come easily.

___ ___ I pay attention and am able to concentrate on assignments.

___ ___ I come to school on time and have good attendance.

___ ___ I am willing to get help on subjects or assignments I don't understand.

___ ___ I work to improve when my grades or test scores are low.

___ ___ I set short and long term goals for myself.

___ ___ In some subjects, I want to do more than just "get by."

___ ___ I am a creative person.

___ ___ I know that doing well in school will help me in the future.

*From **Becoming An Achiever: A Student Guide** by Carolyn Coil. Pieces of Learning, Beavercreek OH*

Personal Characteristics of Students Who Are Becoming Achievers...

Rate your strengths and weaknesses in these areas. Check S for each of your strengths. Then count the number of S's. Check W for weaknesses, but do not check more W's than S's. You may leave some items blank!

S   W

___ ___ I have confidence in myself.

___ ___ I let my teachers know when I am having a problem and work with them in problem solving.

___ ___ I am a risk taker.

___ ___ I am willing to work to make changes in myself.

___ ___ I listen to those in authority over me.

___ ___ I take responsibility for my problems and do not put all of the blame on others.

___ ___ I work well in a group which is working on a constructive project.

___ ___ I have a close friend or friends who share similar positive interests.

___ ___ I am flexible and can see more than one possible solution when solving a problem.

___ ___ I have an area of special interest.

___ ___ I practice self-discipline and self-control.

___ ___ I use my influence over others in a positive way.

___ ___ I have a positive attitude toward school.

___ ___ I know when I have contributed to a behavior problem or conflict.

___ ___ My friends are achievers and have positive attitudes about school

___ ___ I try to have appropriate behavior.

*From **Becoming An Achiever: A Student Guide** by Carolyn Coil. Pieces of Learning, Beavercreek OH*

Presentations, Projects, Performance Samples

Three elements of an effective performance assessment task include:

• A meaningful context in which knowledge is used in a setting important to the student

• Higher level thinking processes where knowledge and skills are applied in a new situation

• An appropriate product or performance which is related to the content

Some examples of performance samples used for assessment include writing, drawing, computations, constructions, and projects. Designing performance assessment tasks helps teachers to focus on what they are expecting students to know and what outcomes they are teaching toward. Performance assessments highlight student work and should promote high-quality performance. This approach usually aligns assessment and instruction because there is an effort to match assessment to student work.

Performance assessments need to include ways for students to reflect about their learning, just as they do when they use journals or portfolios. One way to do this is to video performances and projects for study and evaluation. This allows students to see things they were not aware of during the performance itself. Videos can also show collaboration (or lack thereof) between various students, including who dominates the group and who does not speak up. A video of a performance assessment can be used as a reflective tool. With video records of various performance assessments, students can develop new insights about their work. They can also examine how their knowledge and skills have grown during the school year.

Developing Assessment Criteria

One of the most difficult tasks for teachers who use alternative assessment methods is developing assessment criteria. It is difficult partly because it seems to be quite subjective. There can be a lot of conscious or unconscious bias in this type of assessment, thus we must make sure that the criteria is fair.

Developing assessment criteria is complicated. Assessing complex tasks requires complex assessment criteria, with each part of the task having its own set of criteria. Assessment criteria must be specific and detailed, carefully defined, clear, and easily communicated. The best approach is to look at generic lists of criteria for various tasks, performances or products and then adapt them to meet the specific needs of your content and your students.

Rubrics

A rubric is a set of scoring guidelines for giving scores to student work. A typical rubric:

• Contains a scale of different possible points to be assigned for varying degrees of mastery.

• States the different traits or criteria to be examined in the product or performance.

• Provides pointers for assessing each of the traits and finding the right place on the scoring scale to which a particular student's work corresponds.

In general, performance levels and standards will range from:

1 = The purpose of the task was not accomplished.

2 = Important purposes were not achieved; work needs redirection.

3 = The purpose was not fully achieved; ineffectual strategies; needs elaboration.

4 = For the most part, the purpose was completed.

5 = The purpose of the task was fully accomplished.

6 = The purpose of the task was fully achieved and extended beyond the task.

The standard of '6' is especially good to use in challenging gifted and high ability students to go beyond the 'A' grade or the 100% score on a test. These students need to be stretched to the limits of their abilities!

Most schools, school districts, and state departments of education have been working on rubrics for various alternative assessment tasks in the recent past. Become familiar with these and then adapt them to best meet your needs.

When working on different performance assessment tasks, students should know exactly what the criteria is and teachers ought to be teaching directly to the criteria if the outcomes of the task are worthwhile. Assessment criteria for performance assessments should never be a mystery to the students. No student should ever have to muse: "I wonder how the teacher is going to grade this project?" Instead, students should be able to tell anyone who asks exactly what the assessment criteria is. In fact, in this situation, teaching toward the assessment becomes a goal.

A good reference that contains numerous lists of assessment criteria for many different types of products and performances is *Thematic Activities for Student Portfolios* by Kathy Balsamo, Pieces of Learning, 1995.

Assessment Criteria*

	1	2	3	4	5	6
Organization						
Clarity of thought						
Process follow-through						
Grammar						
Thoroughness						
Resources						
Time Management						
Understanding						
Creativity						
Quality of Presentation						

* From *Thematic Activities for Student Portfolios* and *Questivities*[TM] Sets 1-8. Pieces of Learning. Beavercreek OH

Assessing Creativity

Many teachers have difficulty in assessing products or performances where creativity is the major outcome or learning goal. Below are some guidelines you may wish to use in assessing elements of the creative process.

Guidelines for Assessing Elements of the Creative Process

When assessing creativity or elements of the creative process, incorporate the guidelines below.

Fluency

☐ The number of ideas generated

☐ The number of ideas generated within a certain time

☐ The increase in the number of ideas generated within a certain time

Flexibility

☐ The number of different categories of ideas generated

☐ The number of times the categories change

Originality

☐ The uniqueness of the idea, performance or product as compared to others in the class or group

☐ The uniqueness of the idea, performance or product as compared to what this student has done in the past

Elaboration

☐ The number of details provided in one response

☐ The complexity of a product or performance

☐ The number of sources and ideas used and synthesized into the final product or performance

Divergent Thinking

☐ The number of plausible answers to the same question

☐ The number of alternative solutions to a given problem

Reporting Student Progress

"These report cards are better because you get more than a letter grade. My teacher writes notes telling all about what I'm doing in school."

"When I bring my report card home, my mom sees what I liked in school and what I did well in. It helps me tell her more about school."

"Goal setting on my report card is really good. It focuses me on what I want to do next."

"I can't wait to get my report card! I get to write about three of my strengths and the special project I am going to work on during my next independent study."

The above quotes come from actual students who receive detailed, anecdotal report cards in addition to letter grades. Report cards, newsletters and conferences can be used along with various forms of authentic assessments to convey student progress to parents. Reporting to parents should include not only number or letter grades but also extensive teacher comments, student self-assessments, year long goals for achievement, action plans for future learning, and assessments of each student's strengths and weaknesses.

Alternative assessment methods lead to exciting new ways of communicating with parents and including them in the educational process. Anecdotal report cards with teacher developed comments can clearly and consistently describe each student's progress in relation to the curriculum. Student created report cards encourage students to self assess their performance and set new goals for learning. Student led portfolio conferences which review their work and give them an opportunity to demonstrate their knowledge are important parts of authentic assessment. Newsletters, home response journals and videos in which students tell their parents what they've done and learned in school are other ways of assessing and opening communication between home and school.

It is true that extra planning and preparation are involved when teachers move beyond traditional report cards and assessments. But it is well worth the effort. Parents, students and teachers get more meaningful and in depth information about what has been learned and about goals for future growth.

Problems and Concerns About Alternative Assessment

Giving students choices often goes hand-in-hand with alternative methods of assessment. Make sure student choices do not interfere with what you are trying to assess. Some options or topics may yield easier projects than others and cannot be assessed in the same way. Make sure the assessment for each choice is clear before the choices are made. For more information about designing student choice activities, see page 11 of this book.

Interdisciplinary tasks are often hard to assess and evaluate unless the teacher can distinguish the level of performance in a variety of content areas. Think through assessment criteria in each content area for each task. For example, if the project is writing and performing a historical monologue, assessment criteria in language arts, history, and performing arts would all be used in assessing this performance.

Performances which result from cooperative group efforts are often harder to assess than the work of individual students. One approach is to include an individual assessment component, though even that is somewhat affected by the group. Self assessment and peer assessment from group members are also helpful in this situation. And in any group project or performance, the ability to work as a team should be one of the assessment criteria.

Alternative assessment methods are more difficult to use in higher stakes assessment involving funding, placement and scholarships because a higher level of objectivity and equity is needed in such situations. While standardized tests will probably remain the norm in these areas, alternative assessment has the potential to enrich and expand the information that assessment in general can provide.

Reflections

* Standardized test scores are seen as an extremely important indicator of student learning in most school districts, yet there is usually a wide gap between what is taught in the classroom and what is assessed by these tests.

* These tests are widely used because they provide data for statewide, national or international comparisons of student progress and student learning.

* Student assessment encompasses much more than test taking.

* Authentic assessment measures assess student performance in context and are alternatives to tests.

* Such assessments generally link directly to classroom instruction.

What you Assess is What You Get!

Set learning goals for your students and assess them directly.

These goals must represent the kinds of student work you value.

They must be consistent with high quality teaching strategies and techniques.

[4] Bennett, Dorothy T., senior research associate at the Center for Children and Technology, Electronic Learning, Jan/Feb 1996.

Alternative or Authentic Assessment

Teacher Reflection Page

An environment which encourages alternative or authentic assessment is described below. Assess yourself and your classroom situation to see which of these you are already doing, which you would like to do more, and which you would like to try for the first time.

Students ...

1. do projects on a regular basis, including multiple projects in the same content or interest area.

2. become involved with problems which require an array of knowledge and good judgment about where and how to use that knowledge.

3. work on problems representative of those found in real life, applying knowledge from a variety of content areas effectively and creatively.

4. know and understand assessment criteria and standards so that they are able to prepare and self-assess with accuracy.

5. evaluate and assess their own work as it progresses and relate it to other work they have done previously.

6. discuss, share and learn from others on a regular basis, including those who are assessing them.

7. have real audiences for products or performances beyond just doing work as a class requirement.

8. strive for constant improvement through continually developing higher standards of excellence and working on tasks that require a quality product or performance.

Chapter 7

PUTTING IT ALL TOGETHER

Questions to Consider

1. What is the relationship between Bloom's taxonomy, learning modalities, learning styles and multiple intelligences?

2. How can I help my students develop higher level thinking skills, creativity and research skills as they work on student choice activities from the Individual Lesson Plan?

In the past six chapters, you investigated the *Individual Student Lesson Plan* format and how to use it to incorporate a variety of subject areas, learning styles, learning modalities or taxonomy levels. We have discussed Multiple Intelligences and looked at ways to plan classroom activities and lessons for each. We have also examined alternative assessment and evaluation criteria. While you may now have some tools to use to work with each of these ideas and concepts individually, in "real life" they often work in concert with one another. For example, you may do a learning activity with your students that is at the Application level of Bloom's taxonomy, is appropriate for a Concrete Random learning style, and uses Visual/Spatial intelligence. We need a way to look at these ideas, synthesizing them so that they can work together.

Look at the **Coil Learning Flowchart** on the next page. It is a visual representation of how these ideas work together:

We begin with the Taxonomy of Educational Objectives. These define the objectives (aims or goals) for doing the activity.

Students gather information in a Visual, Verbal, Kinesthetic or Technological mode.

In doing this, they use any combination of the multiple intellegences.

This information is then processed through one of the four learning styles.

The result is a Product, Process and/or Performance.

Then define the educational outcomes through Bloom's taxonomy.

> "A true test of intellectual ability requires the performance of exemplary tasks."
>
> Grant Wiggins

Coil Learning Flowchart™

Aims & Goals for Learning

Taxonomy of Educational Objectives → in Key Subject Areas

Knowledge, Comprehension, Application, Analysis, Synthesis, Evaluation

Gather information through Learning Modalities
Visual, Verbal, Kinesthetic, Technological

Using Multiple Intelligences

Product
Process
Performance

→

Educational Outcomes
Knowledge
Comprehension
Application
Analysis
Synthesis
Evaluation

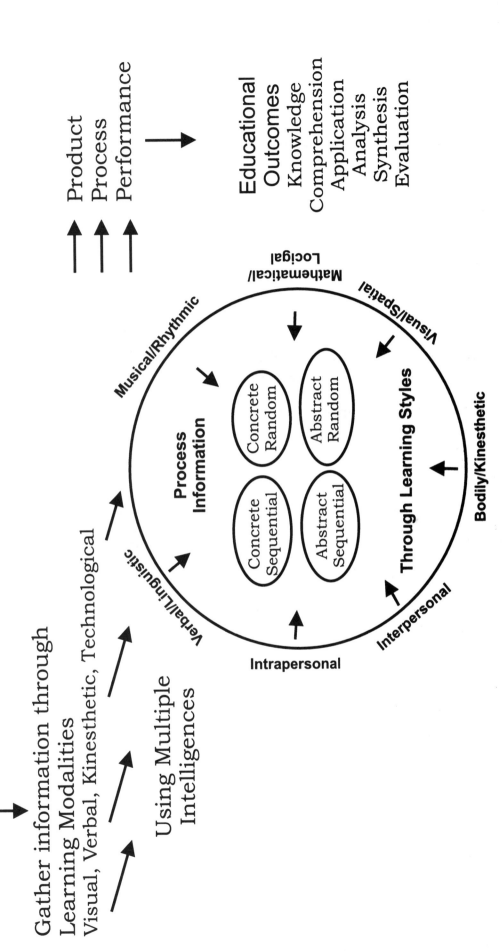

Process Information

Through Learning Styles

Concrete Random
Abstract Random
Concrete Sequential
Abstract Sequential

Musical/Rhythmic
Mathematical/Logical
Visual/Spatial
Bodily/Kinesthetic
Interpersonal
Intrapersonal
Verbal/Linguistic

Writing Questivities™

Using the Questivities™ format is another way to synthesize these ideas. Begin with one of the Student Choice Activities from any of the *Individual Student Lesson Plans* found in this book, or develop your own. Depending upon which format you use, you will already have the learning modality, learning style, subject area or taxonomy level for the activity. For example, if I use the *Individual Student Lesson Plan* on page 42, one of the student choice activities listed in the Kinesthetic modality is:

Make a contraption from paper and show how it works.

I can also identify the following about this activity:

Learning style
Concrete Random

Taxonomy
Application, Analysis

Multiple Intelligence(s)
Bodily/Kinesthetic,
Logical/Mathematical;
Visual/Spatial

The next step is to choose assessment criteria. While there are any number of potential criteria for this activity, for this example I have decided upon:

Assessment
Originality/Creativity
Ability of object to function

The Questivities™ format includes a *Project Question*. This is a broad question that provides an overall focus for doing the project activity.

The Questivities™ (Questioning Activities) are starter questions for students working on the project. They encourage higher level thinking and creativity by guiding and broadening students' thinking as they brainstorm possible answers. The Questivities™ promote research skills by taking students beyond just working on the project itself to thinking about it in a broader context. The Questivities™ are created from a group of phrases which lead to productive questions.

Finally, an *Active Question* is included. This activity promotes higher level thinking skills because in working with an Active Question, students must create a series of their own questions. These, in turn, may create new activities for the thematic unit. An Active Question is written in the following way:

Make a list of questions _____ might ask _____.

Most of the time the blanks are two inanimate objects. In my example, I have asked, "Make a list of questions *a roll of wallpaper* might ask *a can of paint*."

Look at the example on the next page to see a completed Questivities™ format. Page 96 is a reproducible blank form that you can use to write your own Questivities.™

> Students don't care how much you know until they know how much you care.
>
> (Paraphrased from Abraham Lincoln)

Inventions & Inventors

Learning Modality
Kinesthetic

Learning Style
Concrete Random

Taxonomy Level
Application, Analysis

Multiple Intelligence
Bodily/Kinesthetic
Logical/Mathematical
Visual/Spatial

Assessment
Originality/Creativity
Ability of object to function

Project Question
How are new things created or invented?

Questivities™

List all the kinds of paper you could use to make your contraption.
Compare/contrast something made from paper with something made from wood.
What would happen if everything in your house was made from paper?
Would you rather work with paper or work with clay?
How would you feel if you could never use any paper at school? What would school be like?
Why do people in Japan use paper for so many things, such as origami, windows on homes, noshigami (money envelopes) etc.?
How could you make your paper contraption look more beautiful?

Active Questioning
Make a list of questions a roll of wallpaper might ask a can of paint.

> Make a contraption from paper and show how it works.

Learning Modality _____

Learning Style _____

Taxonomy Level _____

Multiple Intelligence _____

Assessment _____

Theme _____

Project activity

Project Question _____

Questivities
List _____

Compare/contrast _____

Would you rather _____

How would you feel if _____

Why _____

How _____

What would happen if _____

Active Questioning
Make a list of questions _____

Reflections

* The Coil Learning Flowchart is a visual representation of how Bloom's Taxonomy, learning modalities, learning styles and Multiple Intelligences work together.

* Questivities™ provide starter questions for students as they work on learning activities and projects. They encourage, stimulate and promote higher level thinking skills, creativity, and research skills.

NOTES

Chapter 8

THE HEART OF TEACHING

Questions to Consider

1. What characteristics make teachers motivational and inspiring to their students?

2. What can I do to make a difference in the lives of my students?

"I don't do very good in school," Tamara confided to me. *"But I think my teachers like me and I know they are trying to help me. One of my teachers takes time every day to make sure I can catch up on my work."*

"Some teachers only care about their subject," complained Wayne. *"They don't care at all about me. When I try to explain anything about what's going on in my life or what's bothering me, they don't even want to listen. They just say, 'That's your problem.' Maybe some things are my problem, but you'd think they would try to help. Most teachers are against the students."*

These two students present two different views of teachers. Their opinions echo the diverse opinions students have of teachers everywhere. As teachers, we can become proficient in all the new educational theories. We can be technically excellent, effective and efficient in our teaching. Yet we may never make any difference in the lives of our students. We need something more, that undefinable emotional element that makes teaching an art, not a science. It is the most important teaching tool of all. I like to call it the heart of teaching.

In my workshops with teachers all over the country I often ask my audience to remember "THE TEACHER" in their lives, that one very special teacher who inspired and motivated them above all others. I find that in an audience of teachers, nearly 90% have had that one special teacher touch their lives in a very profound way. For many, this one special teacher is THE REASON they decided to become teachers themselves.

This was certainly my experience. I was fortunate to have many good, even excellent, teachers during my school years. But there was one who motivated and inspired me, who touched my heart in a very special way with her caring and her love, and had such an impact on my life that even today I would say she is one of the major influences in making me the person I am. This special teacher is Mrs. Mary C. Walker, who was my teacher in junior high school.

When I was in junior high, I thought long and hard about the meaning of teaching and what being a good teacher was really all about. I wrote these thoughts to my special teacher and gave them to her in the middle of an average busy school day. Almost forty years went by. This past summer Mrs. Walker sent my paper, now yellowed with age, back to me. I had totally forgotten about writing it, but she had kept it all these years! As I read it I realized I still feel essentially the same about the true meaning of teaching. Here are the words I wrote:

A Good Teacher

A good teacher likes to teach, likes what she teaches and loves those she teaches.

A good teacher sees each child as an important person, not as a 'thing' for psychiatric analysis or a 'thing' that must be taught.

A good teacher sees herself as an instrument of God — one who is learning through her children rather than the one who knows everything and must teach it to someone who doesn't know as much as she does.

A good teacher finds enjoyment in merely being with her children, sharing their joys and woes and sharing with them a relationship in which learning goes not only from her to them, but from them to her, too.

Mrs. Walker

Carolyn Coil   Age 13

Psychiatrist Dr. Robert Coles suggests that teachers can reach the hearts of their students by sharing their own stories, memories, passions and interests.[5]

Schools must deal with both the head and the heart. If we reach the hearts of our students, we can then awaken their minds. Students who receive insufficient positive attention from peers and adults in school will either fade into the woodwork so that they become essentially invisible, or they will act out and get attention even by negative means. These students are truly "at risk." It is only a matter of time before they will drop out mentally and probably physically as well.

The greatest need of all students is to know we value and love them. Students need to recognize that teachers care about them as individuals. Successful, high achieving students usually feel this way, but other students often do not. What can we do about that? We can take a genuine interest in all of our students, really caring about each of them. Each of us can be a teacher with heart!

Reflections

* Teaching is more than proficiency and efficiency in implementing educational theories and techniques. There is an emotional element in teaching which we can call the HEART of teaching.

* Students must know that we truly care about them, that we value and love them, and that we have a genuine interest in their lives.

[5] ASCD Update, Vol. 35, Number 5, June 1993.

Movies and Videos
That Show the Heart of Teaching

Christy
Dangerous Minds
Dead Poets Society
Fame
Goodbye, Mr. Chips
Good Morning Miss Dove
How Green Was My Valley . .
Little Man Tate
Man Without a Face
Mr. Holland's Opus
Stand and Deliver
To Sir, With Love

The HEART of Teaching

Teacher Reflection Page

Share your thoughts about the heart of teaching with at least one of your colleagues.

Think about your school days. Who was your favorite teacher? What were the things you particularly liked about him or her?

What affective or emotional characteristics make a good teacher? What personal characteristics do students respond to?

What personal characteristics do you have which make you a good teacher? How can you enhance these?

What personal characteristics do you have which detract from your effectiveness as a teacher? How can you minimize them?

How have your views on teaching changed since your school days? Which have remained essentially the same?

What emotional and personal needs do your students have? With which of these needs do you feel most able to help?

Chapter 9

Cultural Diversity

Questions to Consider

1. In what ways is cultural diversity a strength? In what ways is it a challenge?

2. How are learning styles and cultural diversity interrelated?

3. Why should curricula and student learning activities include multicultural themes and concepts?

My mother's parents were both first generation German-American, as their parents emigrated to America from Germany in the late 1800's and subsequently had children who met and married. My father's mother was of English descent and his father was Dutch. When I was a child, I used to proudly declare, "I am an English/Dutch/German American!" I am married to a man whose father had Irish roots and whose maternal grandparents came from Scotland. Our children, then, are Scotch/Irish/English/Dutch/German Americans! Each family has its own saga of diversity. The stories and histories of America's families are witnesses to the cultural diversity that is everywhere in our country.

Cultural diversity is one of the great strengths of our country. We have always been a nation of many cultures and national origins. Our stores and restaurants have products and foods from all over the world; our music, visual and performing arts and popular culture contain a rich variation of ethnic offerings; our styles and fashions have a multitude of origins.

Our diversity, however, also presents one of the biggest challenges for 21st century teachers. Cultural and ethnic differences can result in misunderstandings, conflict and violence. Teaching students from a variety of cultural backgrounds can be difficult at best. Historically, different ethnic groups have been separate from one another, but this is rapidly changing. A multicultural mix of student populations is now found in city, suburban, small town and rural schools. It has become increasingly important to include everyone, to have enough resources to go around, and to ensure equity without sacrificing excellence.

Consider these facts about the year 2000:

- 1 out of every 3 children in school will be an ethnic minority.

- Most students will have roots in more than one ethnic group.

- Urban centers in the Southeast and southwest will double the number of Asian-Pacific students they had in 1990.

- Schools in all parts of the country will have students who do not speak English. [6]

New Immigrants

Recent demographic changes present us with new challenges as we enter the 21st century. The United States is becoming a nation of increasing ethnic and cultural diversity. This trend is affecting schools across America, from urban areas to the traditionally more homogeneous suburbs and small towns. Although the total number of children in our country remained nearly the same between 1980 and 1990, the racial and ethnic composition of school age children changed dramatically. According to the most recent population projections, this trend toward greater and greater cultural diversity will continue well into the 21st century.

With an influx of new non-English speaking immigrants in many schools, teachers may face many students who do not speak English well enough to follow the standard curriculum. In 1995, nationwide, of the 43.6 million children attending public school, nearly one out of every six spoke a language other than English at home, and 2.6 million spoke no English at all. This is an increase of 76% since 1985. Predictions are for this trend to continue beyond the year 2000. What tools can we use to best assimilate and teach these students? [7]

Some research studies indicate that children learn English faster and are more likely to excel academically if they have several years of instruction in their native language first. However, the highest achievers are bilingual students in "two way" schools where English-language children and non-English speakers are together, with half the curriculum taught in a foreign language and half taught in English. Some schools can provide these specialized and highly effective bilingual services, but many cannot or do not. [8]

Language development is not the only concern in teaching immigrant students. Many of these students even at age 12 or 13 have never been to school at all. Because they are not familiar with the American way of life, many immigrant students and their parents are not familiar with the structure and culture of schooling, either. They do not understand such things as how to enroll in school or even how the school calendar works.

Cultural Diversity and Learning Styles

Culture affects learning style and learning modality preferences. To help culturally diverse students achieve, teachers need to use a variety of teaching styles consistent with their students' learning styles. The lesson planning formats found in the first part of this book will be helpful tools in structuring classroom activities that meet the needs of students from diverse cultural backgrounds in the 21st century.

Students from different cultures do learn differently. There are some valid generalizations about differences in learning style from culture to culture, though individual students within each cultural group may differ from one another.

Some cultures are structured so that learning takes place holistically rather than in small separate parts. Students from these cultures have difficulty in the traditional classroom where knowledge is broken into parts rather than looked at as a whole.

Students from African American and Hispanic cultures tend to be field sensitive learners. This means that the social and personal climate of the classroom is important to their learning and that they learn best when they have a personal relationship with the teacher and can interact with their peers.

Students from Asian and Western European backgrounds come from cultures that emphasize field independent learning, that is, learning independently and not involving emotions in the learning situation. This type of student may love doing independent study with little teacher guidance or peer interaction.

Hispanic students come from cultures where families value unity and interdependence within the extended family and where the family highly respects traditions. This culture has a flexible sense of time and uses physical closeness and emotional intensity during conversation.

Asian students also have strong extended family connections and an orientation toward tradition. Their culture respects authority and structure and values silence and privacy. They have a preference for modesty, reserve and self control and a hesitancy about spontaneity and creative thinking.

African American students have strong "in group" values, a group world view, and prefer a call/response style of communication. Their culture shows emotional intensity and expression in oral communication and they prefer spontaneity, physical expression and creative thinking.

Students from Western European cultural backgrounds come from cultures that value individualism, competitiveness, and the nuclear rather than the extended family. They prefer order, control, and logic rather than emotion and spontaneity in responses and decision making.

"The future belongs to those who believe in the beauty of their dreams."

Eleanor Roosevelt

Cultural Diversity

Teacher Reflection Page

1. Trace your own ethnic and cultural roots. List some cultural characteristics that you possess from each group. (For example, family traditions, music, food, memorabilia, etc.)

2. America has been called "A Nation of Immigrants" and "A Melting Pot." Jesse Jackson recently has labeled us a patchwork quilt. Think of a metaphor that most aptly describes your class or your school. Invite your students to brainstorm with you.

3. List the cultural and ethnic groups represented by your students. You may be surprised at how many of your students come from a variety of cultural backgrounds. Look at the cultural characteristics discussed on the previous page. Which characteristics best describe which students?

Student(s)   Cultural Characteristic

4. What is your biggest problem or concern in working with a culturally diverse group of students? Write your problem in the space below. Find strategies to help solve this problem as you read the remainder of this chapter.

Rating Scale for Success in a Culturally Diverse Learning Environment

The conditions and attitudes listed below are important in creating an optimum learning environment for a culturally diverse group of students. Think about your own school and/or classroom situation. Then use the Rating Scale below to see how well your school is equipped to meet the needs of culturally diverse learners.

1= Do not have this at all   2= Seldom   3= Sometimes   4= Often   5= Always

_____ 1.   Equal opportunities for all students to learn

_____ 2.   Cultural awareness among students, parents, educators & support staff.

_____ 3.   Opportunities for community interaction with the school where people from a mix of cultural backgrounds are involved

_____ 4.   Uncrowded classrooms where individual needs can be met

_____ 5.   Qualified educators with an openness to cultural diversity

_____ 6.   Appropriate enrichment materials that reflect a variety of cultures

_____ 7.   Social relationships among peers, educators, and support staff.

_____ 8.   Shared decision making both in individual classrooms and throughout the school

_____ 9.   Multicultural curriculum and instruction

_____ 10.   Opportunities to develop problem solving, cooperative and interpersonal skills

Scoring	
50-41	You are in a school where students from all cultures should do very well
40-31	Your school has many attributes for success with cultural diversity
30-21	You have some positive elements in working with culturally diverse students, but there is room for improvement
20-11	Your school needs to make the needs of cultural diverse students a top priority.
10-0	Your school needs to examine ways to meet the needs of all students and then make a plan for implementation.

Strategies for Working with Culturally Diverse Students

Teachers should know the essential elements of their students' cultural backgrounds and know how to interpret their students' behavior from a cultural perspective. Below are some specific strategies that will help you to work with culturally diverse students.

1. Talk with your students to find out more about their culture.

2. Respect the cultural knowledge of your students; become a learner of their cultural ideas!

3. Consult a school counselor or ESL specialist in your school district to learn more about the various cultures of your students.

4. Encourage students to write about their experiences and the places they have lived.

5. Use advisory committees with members who represent a variety of cultures.

6. Develop partnerships with local businesses who are successful in serving people from a variety of cultures.

7. During discussion times, use terminology from a variety of cultures.

8. State items in a positive manner when correcting oral language. Use phrases such as "Let's say" instead of "Don't say it that way!"

9. Assess each child's strengths as well as his or her weaknesses. *

10. Modify thematic units, classroom materials and activities to include a variety of cultures.

11. Adapt materials to make the language simpler but do not "water down" the content.

12. Use graphic organizers, diagrams and drawings to aid students in identifying concepts and seeing relationships.

13. Use visual aids, demonstrations and hands-on learning when teaching significant concepts.

14. Have culturally diverse magazines, books, newspapers, etc. available as classroom resources.

15. Take advantage of workshops, seminars, university courses, international organizations, tours and exchange programs, and one-on-one conversations with people from different cultures to increase your own cultural awareness.

* (See ***Motivating Underachievers*** and ***Becoming an Achiever*** by Carolyn Coil for useful assessment tools.)

Strategies for Working with Families of Culturally Diverse Students

Knowing about the cultural background of the families of your students is extremely important, especially in a school that includes several different cultures. Below are some strategies to consider as you work with the families of your students.

1. Invite parents to visit the school before their child is enrolled. Try to make them feel at home in the school setting.

2. Be sure to **listen carefully** to parents to develop an understanding of their values and beliefs.

3. Invite parents to participate in school programs in any way it is convenient to their individual schedules.

4. Talk to parents about volunteering in school and sharing information and customs about their culture with all students. Do this on a small scale at first so you don't frighten them!

5. Identify all of the significant adults for the child within the family structure. This is particularly important in cultures with large extended families.

6. Encourage parents to bring an interpreter to conferences and/or try to locate interpreters for parents who do not speak English.

7. Have an all-school talent show or other event where parents can see their children working in partnership with children of other cultures.

8. Make phone calls or have conferences with parents explaining school procedures in areas such as report cards, testing or other means of assessment, school awards, school programs, etc. Parents may be totally unaware of many of these procedures.

9. Plan and implement schoolwide or classroom ethnic-oriented social events. Enlist parent help.

10. Make print materials available to parents in their native language. Find a volunteer or business partner who will help you.

Multicultural Teaching

"Multicultural education is simply teaching people about other cultures, starting with the cultures they encounter every day. We want students to know about the cultures surrounding them and the cultures they may encounter later in life."

— Bruce Davis, Elementary School Principal, Rosemead, California

As we approach the 21st century, most educators realize that all students need to learn not only about their own culture but also about the cultures of others; for they either live at present — or in the future will live — in a multicultural environment. Schools need to teach not only about various cultures around the world, but also about the various cultures within our own country and our own communities.

Curricula are continuing to expand to include the cultures of the many diverse groups that make up the United States. For the most part, multicultural education has been included in the content areas of social studies, history, and literature, and in interdisciplinary thematic units. As teachers who are preparing students for the 21st century, you need to develop proficiency in designing lessons from a multicultural perspective, thereby teaching your students about other cultures in the world. The challenge is to create an environment that is respectful of different cultures, but at the same time, maintain a common culture within your school or classroom that everyone can identify with.

Thematic units are tools that work well in teaching students multicultural concepts and key ideas such as immigration, language, intercultural relations, holidays and celebrations, myths and folk tales, conflict, etc. Use different activities related to a specific theme to help your students see a variety of perspectives. For example, have them participate in role playing, with various students showing differing perspectives through the roles they have taken on. This will help your students become critical thinkers as they see different sides to an issue or question.

On the next page, you will see a sample thematic unit entitled "We Are Multicultural" which can be used to increase multicultural understanding. Page 111 shows how the *Individual Student Lesson Plan* format can be used to give students choices in the learning activities based on this theme and how to develop Questivities™ (page 112) to further your students' multicultural understanding. On page 113 there is a Visual Organizer for Compare/Contrast activities. Page 114 is a blank form for your use. (Page 113 shows how this form was used by students to compare and contrast three ethnic groups.) You may wish to adapt or modify these to better suit the specific needs and/or cultural origins of your students.

> Differences in language and culture can cause conflict between the home and the school.
>
> –Baca and Cervantes

We Are Multi-Cultural

Make a chart comparing and contrasting at least two cultures represented by students in your class.

Demonstrate/explain a sport, dance, or cultural event from another country.

Take a survey of ethnic foods people eat. Generate a graph showing results.

Make a list of at least 25 English words that come from other languages. Explain why they are part of the English language.

Make a list of questions you have about another country. Post on a computer bulletin board. Record the answers you receive.

View a video from another culture. Make a compare/contrast chart of your culture with the culture in the video.

Make a list of holidays from a variety of cultures. Make an illustrated encyclopedia of these holidays.

Share a folktale from another culture with your class. Dress in costume.

Make a poster showing what people from a variety of cultures think is "beautiful."

Make a large world map labeling the ethnic and cultural origins of the students in your class.

Role play some problems a non-English speaking student might have at your school.

Wear the native costume of another culture. Explain its meaning and function.

INDIVIDUAL LESSON PLAN - Learning Modalities

ACTIVITIES - STUDENT CHOICES

Visual

1. Make a list of holidays from a variety of cultures. Make an illustrated encyclopedia of these holidays.
2. Make a large world map labeling the ethnic/cultural origins of the students in your class.
3. Make a chart comparing and contrasting at least two cultures represented by students in your class.

Verbal

7. Share a folktale from another culture with your class. Dress in costume.
8. Role play some problems a non-English speaking student might have at your school.
9. Make a list of at least 25 English words that come from other languages. Explain why they are part of the English language.

Kinesthetic

4. Make a poster showing what people from a variety of cultures think is "beautiful."
5. Wear the native costume of another culture. Explain its meaning & function.
6. Demonstrate/explain a sport, dance, or cultural event from another country.

Technological

10. Survey ethnic foods people eat. Generate a graph showing results.
11. Make a list of questions you have about another country. Post on a computer bulletin board. Record the answers.
12. View a video from another culture. Make a compare/contrast chart of your culture with the culture in the video.

Required Activities
Teacher's Choice

1. Make a family tree showing your family's origins.
2. On a world map, identify and color code the countries of your ancestors' origins.
3. Read a book that is set in another culture or one about a person from another culture. Summarize the book in a short illustrated report.

Product/Performance
Required

1. Family Tree
2. Map

3. Illustrated report

Assessment
Required Activities

1. Accurate visual Visually pleasing
2. Accurate labeling of countries
3. Report reflects cultural differences Illustration compliments written report

---

Optional
Student-Parent
Cooperative Activity

Interview a relative or family friend from another culture. Use an audio or video tape to record your interview.

Student Choices in
Ways to Learn

Visual
2
___

Verbal
6
___

Kinesthetic
9
___

Technological
10
___

Product/Performance
Student Choice

2. Map

6. Demonstration

9. List of words

10. Graph

Assessment
Student Choice

2. All students included; accurate geographically
6. Knowledge of item demonstrated
9. Accuracy; variety of words
10. Appropriate visual; correct information

©1997 Carolyn Coil and Pieces of Learning

We Are Multi-Cultural

Make a large world map and label the ethnic/cultural origins of all the students in your class.

Learning Modality
Visual

Learning Style
Concrete Sequential

Taxonomy Level
Knowledge, Comprehension

Multiple Intelligence
Visual/Spatial
Interpersonal

Assessment
1. Includes all students
2. Accurate geographically

Project Question
What are the ethnic/cultural origins of the students in your class?

Questivities™

List all the students in your class and at least one ethnic/cultural group for each.
Compare/contrast characteristics of two different ethnic/cultural groups.
Would you rather be friends with people just like you or with people different from you?
How would you feel if you were told your ethnic/cultural group was totally bad? totally perfect?
Why do some people dislike people who are different from them?
How can you help your classmates avoid prejudice?
What would happen if everyone in your school came from just one culture?

Active Questioning
Make a list of questions a new immigrant from Bosnia might ask the Statue of Liberty.

A Visual Organizer for Compare/Contrast Activities

Ethnic Groups in Our Class

Below are topics to consider when comparing and contrasting each group. Some information has been filled in for each item. Your students may be able to add more. Have students continue to list similarities and differences.

When did this group come to America?

Asian-American	African American	Native American
Chinese immigrants 1850 Japanese immigrants 1900 Southeast Asian immigrants 1973-1990s	Through the slave trade from the early 1700's to 1865	From Asia over Bering Strait land bridge 20,000 years ago

What are some important contributions?

Asian-American	African American	Native American
Completion of railroad east to west Engineering, math, science	Fight for civil rights and desegregation Sports, music, literature, politics	Foods such as corn and squash Love of the environment and the land Survival skills

Instances of unfair treatment

Asian-American	African American	Native American
Internment of Japanese during WWII	Slavery Discrimination Segregation in schools and housing	Land taken away Cherokee Trail of Tears Treaties broken

A Visual Organizer for Compare/Contrast Activities

When students are asked to do a Compare/Contrast activity, this visual organizer should help them to more easily see similarities and differences. First, brainstorm questions or topics that could be considered in comparing and contrasting. Write each on the appropriate line on the visual organizer. Then fill in the information for each item. From this students will be able to list similarities and differences.

Question or topic

Item 1	Item 2	Item 3

Question or topic

Item 1	Item 2	Item 3

Question or topic

Item 1	Item 2	Item 3

Some Final Thoughts About Multicultural Education

Multicultural education should not divide students. Instead it should be a tool to use in uniting your students who come from such diverse backgrounds. The goal is to create authentic unity that reflects an understanding of all your students' experiences. Begin by examining differences but emphasize what we all have in common. Schools must show both our country's unity and its diversity.

There is no need to put emphasis on victimization or on how a minority culture has been victimized by the majority culture. At the same time, you don't want to avoid controversial issues within a culture such as racism, prejudice and inequality.

Young children, especially, need to see the positive accomplishments of people from a variety of cultures. Avoid stereotypes by instead describing some global characteristics of various ethnic groups. There is a fine line between generalizing and stereotyping. Generalizations are necessary for the study of groups because they give us clues to what individuals were like and how and why they acted as they did. Stereotypes give absolute answers or negative impressions with few facts or examples to back them up.

There is no doubt that multicultural education can lead to a discussion of issues that can be divisive and may cause conflict. Here are some guidelines to follow when an area of conflict arises:

Guidelines for Managing Multicultural Discussions and Conflicts

1. Set parameters for the discussion before it begins.

2. Keep the discussion factual not emotional.

3. Help the class work through a conflict or misunderstanding by discussing it rationally.

4. Be a good listener and moderator for the discussion.

5. Be clear that everything presented about various cultures does not have to be tolerated or valued on a personal level.

6. Do not allow the discussion to evolve into name calling.

7. Remind your students that understanding begins with listening to another's point of view.

8. Limit the time to be spent in discussion of a particular issue before the discussion begins.

For further information about conflict management, see Chapter 12.

Reflections

* The cultural diversity of our students is, paradoxically, one of our greatest strengths while it provides one of the greatest challenges for 21st century teachers.

* Valid generalizations can be made about the learning style preferences of each cultural group. However, stereotyping should be avoided. Individual students within each cultural group can and do differ from one another.

* Students living in a multicultural environment need to explore lessons with multicultural themes to learn multicultural concepts and about the cultures represented by their classmates and neighbors.

[6] "The Fabric of a Nation," Modern Maturity, June-July, 1992.

[7] Time magazine, Special Issue, Fall, 1993.

[8] ASCD Update, Vol. 36, Number 5, June, 1994.

"America is not like a blanket -- one piece of unbroken cloth, the same color, the same texture, the same size. America is more like a quilt -- many pieces, many colors, many sizes, all woven and held together by a common thread."

Jesse Jackson

Chapter 10

Inclusion of Children With Disabilities

Questions to Consider

1. What beliefs support the idea of inclusion?

2. Why is inclusion becoming more and more commonplace in American schools?

3. How does inclusion work successfully?

4. What problems and concerns are there about the inclusion process?

Bart is an emotionally disturbed fifth grader. His achievement test scores in both reading and math are below grade level. Yet he often displays lots of intelligence when he writes science fiction stories and draws cartoon illustrations to match. His plots and characters are well developed and show a great deal of creativity, though his grammar and spelling need improvement. Because the regular education teacher works collaboratively with the special education teacher, Bart receives the assistance he needs to keep his behavior under control. Bart can function well included in a regular classroom setting.

Janine has a learning disability. She is in eighth grade but has difficulty in reading and with organizational skills. She is easily distracted and has characteristics of ADD, though she has never been formally diagnosed as having it. Janine is in a middle school committed to the philosophy of inclusion. The special education teacher is one of five teachers on the middle school

team. She works with the four subject area teachers in planning curriculum, teaching strategies and lessons, adapting and modifying materials, and working with groups of students who need special help. Janine, along with several other of her disabled and non-disabled classmates, meets with the special ed teacher for a study skills seminar twice a week. Occasionally, Janine also has a time scheduled for some individual tutoring.

Due to an educational practice known as *inclusion*, Bart and Janine, though identified as students with disabilities, are receiving their education in the regular classroom setting. Inclusion is an educational philosophy based on the belief that entitles all students to participate fully in their school community. The term usually refers to the commitment to educate each child, to the maximum extent appropriate, in the school and classroom the student would attend if the disabling condition were not present.

Inclusion has come about due to the belief that children with disabilities who are segregated into special education classrooms are receiving education that is inherently unequal. Many children who have been in special education programs have not developed necessary academic, vocational or social skills. Inclusion moves such students, along with support services, into the regular classroom.

The inclusion of students with disabilities into the regular classroom has become increasingly common throughout the United States. Federal laws require that schools make a significant effort to find an inclusive setting for the delivery of educational services to students with disabilities.

> **The Individuals with Disabilities Education Act** states: "Unless a handicapped child's individualized education program requires some other arrangement, the child is educated in the school which he or she would attend if not handicapped." **Section 504 of the Rehabilitation Act of 1973** requires: "A recipient of federal funds...shall educate, or shall provide for the education of, each qualified handicapped person in its jurisdiction with persons who are not handicapped to the maximum extent appropriate to the needs of the handicapped person."

In the past few years, federal court cases have interpreted these laws to require the inclusion of children with disabilities, even severe disabilities, in the school and classroom they would attend if they were not disabled. Even if they cannot keep up with the academic work, the courts have decided these students must be included if there is a potential social benefit.

An inclusion model involves a disabled child being placed in a regular classroom to the maximum extent appropriate. The aim of inclusion is to integrate the students, along with the supports they need, into classrooms with non-disabled peers. It involves bringing the support services to the child and requires that the child will benefit from this in some way (academically, socially, and/or emotionally).

The most common support services are consultation and training for the regular classroom teacher. In schools where inclusion works well, the regular classroom teacher has continual access to and communication with a support staff who can help find equipment and materials and help modify teaching techniques to meet the needs of disabled students. Necessary supports in terms of equipment and trained personnel are also necessary for the related medical services needed by some disabled children.

Elements of Successful Inclusion

When inclusion works well, children with disabilities become members of their classroom communities, valued for their abilities and for who they are. In a fully inclusive school, the term 'special education' is rarely used. Proponents of "full inclusion" believe that it should be the regular classroom teacher's responsibility to educate children with disabilities.

The regular classroom teacher must learn how to adapt the classroom to accommodate the child with a disability and needs the necessary technical assistance. In an ideal inclusive classroom, the regular teacher and a support specialist work together in an arrangement that best meets an individual student's needs. This can range from occasional technical support to full-time classroom assistance.

In an inclusion model, disabled students sometimes leave the regular classroom to receive support services, but they do not leave just because they are learning at a different rate or with different materials from their classmates.

The major benefits of inclusion for disabled children are higher academic expectations and accomplishments and the development of better socialization skills. There are benefits for non-disabled children, too, who learn to accept human differences. They often grow academically as a result of collaborative teaching and the use of innovative teaching strategies and regular classroom techniques. Inclusion gives all students broad opportunities to interact with a variety of people. Non-disabled students can develop a sense of responsibility and increased self esteem when working with disabled classmates.

One of the main advantages for non-disabled students is that they can learn to overcome their stereotypes, prejudices and misconceptions about students with disabilities. Teachers in an inclusive classroom must not allow disabled students to become the source of jokes or victims of teasing and ridicule. This is one of the major problems for disabled students in a regular classroom setting.

At the end of this chapter is a sample unit entitled "Understanding Disabilities" that increases understanding and helps students overcome misconceptions about disabilities. *The Individual Student Lesson Plan* format gives students choices in the learning activities based on this theme. The sample Questivities show how to develop each activity to further students' understanding of disabilities and their disabled classmates.

Successful inclusion takes time. Schools need to establish it gradually. Teachers need time to talk with one another and work out strategies for dealing with disabled children. Collaboration with specialists and receiving adequate training to work with disabled children are two necessary elements for a successful inclusion program. When regular education and special education teachers can work in teams, when there is a full and equal partnership between the teachers, and when they plan lessons together and collaborate to individualize instruction, inclusion is much more likely to work.

Inclusion works best when it is part of several other reforms such as team teaching, peer teaching, cooperative learning, authentic assessment, multiage classes, middle school structures, access to innovative technology and thematic interdisciplinary instruction. It thrives where there is good communication, a culture of innovation, and a philosophy of individualization for all students. When inclusion works best, all teachers are collaborating and learning new skills that in turn benefit all students.

"The test of a first-rate intelligence is the ability to hold two opposing ideas in the mind at the same time and still retain the ability to function."

F. Scott Fitzgerald

Strategies for Beginning a Successful Inclusion Program

Teacher Reflection Page

Before beginning an inclusion program and at the beginning of each school year, discuss and act upon the issues listed below. Take time to discuss these items with your colleagues.

1. Schedule planning and collaboration time. Special education and regular education teachers need time to share concerns and areas of expertise. This cannot be done in five minutes while walking down the hallway!

2. Consider your own attitude and the attitudes of other teachers regarding disabled students have their needs met, and communicate the benefits of inclusion for them to their parents.

3. Look at students with disabilities as people first. Concentrate on other attributes rather than the disability. For example, instead of saying, "My deaf student" refer to the student as "My student who loves cats" or "My student who can never find a pencil." All students with disabilities have other attributes besides the disability.

4. Be willing to collaborate with and teach with another teacher. You must adjust and compromise on some things, but you will learn many new things from your colleague, too.

5. Don't be afraid to ask for help. Contrary to popular opinion, this is not a sign of weakness. Other professionals routinely consult colleagues, especially about difficult cases. Teachers should do the same.

6. Discuss logistics such as scheduling, paperwork, use of materials, ways of grouping students, etc. Decide the 'nuts and bolts' issues ahead of time. When teaching with another teacher, watch for gaps and overlaps. A gap occurs when each of you assumes the other is responsible for a given task and the task does not get done. An overlap occurs when both of you do the same task that only needed to be done once.

7. Visit other classrooms and other schools to see how they are implementing inclusion. You will get some good ideas and will learn from their mistakes. There is no need to "reinvent the wheel"; learn from others!

8. Make sure the non-disabled students have their needs met, and communicate the benefits of inclusion for them to their parents.

Problems and Concerns About Inclusion

The negative aspects of inclusion include the fact that teachers receive inadequate resources and are excluded from planning how to work with these disabled students. Some teachers report that suddenly several disabled students are "dumped" into their classes and that they have had no training in how to deal with them. It is easy to see why teachers feel resentful of such a practice!

Ideally, every school that decides to implement inclusion would supply all of the assistance teachers need to make it successful. However, some schools begin inclusion without the needed supports, and when the support and resources are not there, terrible problems can develop. For example, IEP's are sometimes withheld from regular teachers though they are responsible for the modifications in instruction and testing stated on the IEP. If regular teachers are not informed about their students' disabilities, disastrous consequences often are the result. When administration provides no training for regular classroom teachers, they rightly feel inadequate and resentful.

Maintaining proper supports for children with disabilities and those who teach them requires a great degree of commitment, communication and skill. Assigning disabled children to regular classrooms because of budget cuts is not the way to make inclusion happen successfully. Inclusion is never merely a cost cutting approach. Nor is it good to have token inclusion that isolates the disabled child in the classroom and provides no peers with a similar special need. Additionally, if a special education teacher has 20 students who are dispersed into 10 different classrooms, it is difficult to see how true collaboration can happen.

Peer tutoring can be a successful strategy in an inclusive classroom. A word of caution — don't overuse it. If it becomes the predominant mode of instruction, this is not beneficial to the student doing the tutoring nor to the disabled student being tutored!

The goal of providing equal educational opportunity through inclusion often comes face to face with the practical concerns of implementing this philosophy in the classroom. Some issues include:

☐ Administrative support

☐ Specialized training

☐ Paraprofessional assistance

☐ Being overwhelmed by the demands of caring for a severely disabled child

☐ Managing an environment filled with even more diverse needs than are already present in a typical classroom

☐ Encouraging diversity and equity yet providing instructional excellence

☐ Participation in inclusion - must all teachers be involved?

☐ Is this just another idea that will fade with time?

☐ Dealing with a student whose behavior is dangerous/disruptive to others

☐ Documenting gains in academic and social skills for disabled students

Discuss these issues in your school!

Magnet Enriched Classrooms: An Inclusion Model That Works

The Kids Are People School, a private preschool / elementary school in Boston, Massachusetts, has successfully integrated "typical needs" and "special needs" children for over 15 years. Both groups, disabled or not, represent diverse backgrounds and intelligences. The director of this school does not believe in "forced inclusion." In fact, she thinks this is the worst thing we can do to children. Instead, in a Magnet Enriched Classroom only those teachers who are comfortable with special needs and who have faith in their abilities to work with such students can apply for the job of inclusion classroom teacher.

Like the magnet schools concept, implementing Magnet Enriched Classrooms within each school (such as the ones described above) involves including both disabled and non-disabled students in an enriched educational environment. The low student/teacher ratio and innovative instructional approaches in this type of classroom appeal to many parents and to non-disabled students who differ in ability just as disabled students do.

Teachers use physical space in innovative ways. Specialists, classroom teachers and paraprofessionals co-teach and have training and planning time together. This model envisions a learning environment filled with ideas, energy and resources. Only teachers who truly want to participate in the inclusion of special needs children are selected for the magnet room assignment.

Magnet classrooms must provide a full menu of choices for students. Such classrooms benefit from a student-centered curriculum characterized by adaptability, flexibility and personalization for each student. They incorporate the ideal of high expectations for all students, with teachers knowing how to "push" and knowing how to praise. In the Magnet Enriched Classroom setting, perseverance is important for both teachers and students.

The "Secret Techniques" Myth

Special education teachers do not possess some secret or magic teaching technique that they use with their students that other teachers know nothing about. Good teachers of special needs students do what good teachers of all students do. They are sensitive to individual problems and needs. They diversify and modify techniques, materials, activities, assignments and assessment.

Special education students are more similar to "regular" students than they are different. Most are just as capable of learning. Students with learning disabilities and behavior disorders, for instance, possess ingenuity, creativity and intelligence as much as any other group of students. Their disabilities have often interfered, but do not have to interfere, with their ability to learn.

Modifying and Adapting Educational Materials and Teaching Techniques

One successful strategy for inclusion is to modify and adapt the materials and teaching techniques you are currently using in your classroom. If you are a regular education teacher, ask the special education teacher to help you. Often special education teachers will have materials they have already adapted and can offer suggestions for new techniques. Making minor alterations can sometimes result in a big difference in the possibilities of success for a student with disabilities. Below are some easily implemented suggestions for modifying and adapting materials and teaching techniques.

1. Present work in smaller amounts. Give students with disabilities smaller increments of work at a time. This helps the student who is overwhelmed by a large assignment.

2. Make a special loose-leaf workbook for your disabled student so that all of his or her papers can be kept in one place.

3. Mark pages that need to be done with a paper clip or self-stick note.

4. Secure work to the student's desk with masking tape.

5. Allow the student to underline or circle answers instead of writing them. Encourage the use of highlighters and other writing tools.

6. If the student has trouble copying items from the board, have the assignment written out for him/her ahead of time.

7. Adapt the amount of work required depending on the pace the student is able to set for the task at hand.

8. Keep materials on a shelf or locker except for the ones the student is currently using.

9. Adjust the physical arrangements of your classroom in any way that might help students with disabilities. This includes knowing the best viewing distance for reading print materials, locations that facilitate hearing and lip reading, adaptations for physical impairments, etc.

10. Provide visual tools such as outlines, mindmaps and other visual organizers that students can use to help direct their thinking.

11. Use technological tools to support learning.
   Adaptive computer devices of all types are available for disabled students.
   Use tape recorders for storytelling, data collection and oral journals.
   Encourage the use of word processors and graphics programs.
   Use VCR's, camcorders, and other tools for multimedia projects.

For more information on technology, see chapter 14. Also, contact the Council for Exceptional Children, Technology and Media Division, 1920 Association Drive, Reston, VA 22091

Strategies for Successful Inclusion

Teacher Reflection Page

Listed below are a number of strategies and techniques to use to build a school and classroom climate where inclusion models can be successfully implemented. Consider each item listed. To what extent does this already exist in your school or classroom? If you are already using it, what could you do differently to increase its effectiveness? If you are not currently using the strategy, how could you begin to implement it?

☐ 1. Hands-on teaching

☐ 2. Combination of child directed and teacher directed activities

☐ 3. Teacher as the facilitator of learning

☐ 4. Multiage classes

☐ 5. Individualized instruction

☐ 6. Cooperative learning

☐ 7. Peer tutoring or buddy system

☐ 8. Modifying and adapting educational materials

☐ 9. Innovative use of classroom space

☐ 10. Use of technological tools

☐ 11. Low child-to-teacher ratio

☐ 12. Alternative assessment

☐ 13. Collaboration between teachers

☐ 14. Using the "Understanding Disabilities" thematic unit found on the next three pages

Disabilities

Write a short story about a day in your life pretending you have a disability or an actual day in your life if you are disabled.

Spend a day in a wheelchair. Demonstrate problems you had.

Demonstrate a technological device that is specifically designed to assist persons with disabilities.

Read a biography about a famous disabled person. Design a book jacket with a picture of the person & summary of his/her life.

Investigate ways technology has allowed persons with disabilities to do many more things. Report your findings to your class.

Learn the braille alphabet. Write a paragraph in braille. Use a braille writer if available at your school.

Make a video of the Special Olympics in your area. Interviews Special Olympics athletes.

Find out about learning disabilities. Explain this disability to your class through a skit or role play.

Make a chart about one type of disability. Include things that persons with this disability CAN do.

On audio tape interview a classmate or someone else in your school with a disability. Find out their challenges and successes.

Learn to sing a song in sign language. Perform the song for your class.

Look for places in your school that are not accessible to physically disabled people. Draw a diagram or plan showing how they could become accessible.

INDIVIDUAL LESSON PLAN - Learning Modalities

ACTIVITIES - STUDENT CHOICES

Visual

1. Make a chart about one type of disability. Include things that persons with this disability CAN do.
2. Look for places in your school that are not accessible to physically disabled people. Draw a diagram or plan showing how they could become accessible.
3. Read a biography about a famous disabled person. Design a book jacket with a picture of the person & summary of his/her life.

Verbal

7. On audio tape interview a classmate or someone else in your school with a disability. Find out their challenges and successes.
8. Write a short story about a day in your life pretending you have a disability or an actual day in your life if you are disabled.
9. Find out about learning disabilities. Explain this disability to your class through a skit or role play.

Kinesthetic

4. Learn to sing a song in sign language. Perform the song for your class.
5. Spend a day in a wheelchair. Demonstrate problems you had.
6. Learn the braille alphabet. Write a paragraph in braille. Use a braille writer if available at your school.

Technological

10. Investigate ways technology has allowed persons with disabilities to do many more things. Report your findings to your class.
11. Demonstrate a technological device that is specifically designed to assist persons with disabilities.
12. Make a video of the Special Olympics in your area. Interviews Special Olympics athletes.

Required Activities
Teacher's Choice

1. Listen to a Special Education teacher talk about types of disabilities and the inclusion model in your classroom. Write your questions about disabilities on index cards.
2. Collect 3 news stories about people with disabilities. Write a summary of each.
3. View the "Kids on the Block" puppet show. Participate in follow-up activities.

Optional
Student-Parent
Cooperative Activity

Find out about a relative with a disability. What are his/her problems? successes? Make a scrapbook about this person.

Student Choices in Ways to Learn

Visual
3

Verbal
4

Kinesthetic
9

Technological
11

Product/Performance
Required

1. Questions on index cards
2. Summary of news stories
3. Follow up activities

Product/Performance
Student Choice

3. Book jacket
4. Sign language performance
9. Skit or role play
11. Demonstration

Assessment
Required Activities

1. Observation from discussion about questions
2. Comprehension of stories
3. Active participation

Assessment
Student Choice

3. Well organized; accurate; artwork complements story
4. accuracy of sign language; expression
9. accuracy of information; preparation; stage presence
11. Equipment working; ability to use; explanation of function

Understanding Disabilities

> Demonstrate a technological device that is specifically designed to assist persons with disabilities. Explain how it works and how it helps a disabled person

Learning Modality
Technological

Learning Style
Concrete Random

Taxonomy Level
Application

Multiple Intelligence
Visual/Spatial
Interpersonal
Bodily/Kinesthetic
Verbal/Linguistic

Assessment
1. Equipment working
2. Ability to use
3. Explanation of function

Project Question
In what ways can technology be used to make life better for people with disabilities?

Questivities™
List all the types of technological devices that may help people with disabilities.
Compare/contrast a battery-run wheelchair with a wheelchair that has no battery.
How is a robot like a guide dog?
What new technological devices could be invented to help persons with disabilities?
Why do some people with disabilities use a head pointer?
How could a technological device help some parapeligics walk again?

Active Questioning
Make a list of all the questions a speech synthesizer might ask a tape recorder.

NOTES

Chapter 11

Educating Gifted Students

Questions to Consider

1. What does gifted mean? Which students are gifted?

2. What types of learning activities do gifted students need?

3. What strategies can I use for the inclusion of gifted students in the regular classroom?

4. Which type of grouping is best to develop a good gifted program?

5. What can school districts do to develop a good gifted program?

Jac is in first grade and has been reading for years. At 18 months he could read labels and signs, and in the summer between kindergarten and first grade he read five volumes of C.S. Lewis' "Chronicles of Narnia" series. Jac's first grade teacher is at a loss about how to teach him.

Shaundra is a 7th grader who is a high achiever. She is a straight A student who works rapidly and invariably completes her assignments before the rest of the class. The teacher often asks her to help by tutoring slower students.

Maria is quite artistic. She is an independent learner who "sneaks" books to read during class but doesn't always finish her assigned work. She doodles when she should be taking notes and draws clever, humorous cartoons that are very popular with her classmates.

Rebellious Greg refuses to do his assigned work in school. He is considered a behavior problem by his teachers and makes poor grades on his report card. Yet he tests in the gifted range on standardized IQ tests. The guidance counselor at his school calls him a "classic underachiever."

Who are the Gifted?

All four of the students described above are gifted, yet they are very different and individualistic in their abilities and educational needs. Gifted students range from the highly gifted to the cooperative "teacher's pet," and from the artist to the rebellious underachiever. No wonder it is difficult to say exactly who gifted students are!

For nearly 40 years, American educators have struggled to define what giftedness means. In 1972, the U.S. Office of Education issued the Marland Report. This report concluded there are at least six categories of gifted and talented children "who by virtue of outstanding abilities are capable of high performance." From this came the Federal law (Public Law 91-230) that defines gifted and talented children in five of the original six categories:

- General intellectual ability

- Specific academic aptitude

- Creative or productive thinking

- Leadership ability

- Visual/performing arts

This law also states:

"These are children who require differentiated educational programs and/or services beyond those normally provided by the regular school programs to realize their contribution to self and society."

States, however, can construct their own definition of giftedness and to decide whether to mandate programs for gifted and talented students. Therefore, you will find great variety in the programs and services offered for gifted students in school districts throughout the United States. You will also discover many different opinions about which students are actually gifted.

For many years, districts identified a disproportionate number of white middle class students as gifted while they did not identify minority students as gifted. Some states have changed their definition of giftedness and their eligibility criteria so that gifted programs are more inclusive. In 1996, the state of Georgia, for example, began including four categories of eligibility for gifted. These are Mental Ability, Achievement, Creativity, and Motivation. A student must meet criteria in three of the four categories to be eligible for gifted programs and services. Before 1996, Georgia only included the category of Mental Ability in its criteria.

Needs of Gifted Students

A "one size fits all" curriculum actually fits no one. This is especially true for gifted and talented students. In order for them to reach their potential so that they can be the leaders in academia, business and the arts in the 21st century, they should work and study hard to master challenging knowledge and skills. Unfortunately, the message gifted students often get is to drift through school and aim for adequacy, not excellence.

According to "National Excellence: A Case for Developing America's Talent," a report issued in 1993 by the U.S. Department of Education, most gifted and talented students spend their school days without having much attention given to their specific learning needs. Consider these findings cited in the report:

- Gifted and talented elementary school students have mastered from 35 to 50 percent of the curriculum offered in five basic subjects before they begin the school year.

- Most regular classroom teachers make few, if any, provisions for gifted and talented students.

- Most of the highest achieving students in the nation included in Who's Who Among American High School Students reported that they studied less than an hour a day.

It is easy to see why so many gifted students say they are bored in school!

INCLUSION STRATEGIES for WORKING WITH GIFTED STUDENTS IN THE REGULAR CLASSROOM

Most gifted students spend the majority of their time in school in the regular classroom setting. Since they are not gifted just when they go to the gifted class (if such a class exists in their school), it is important that all educators have the tools to meet their needs through the learning activities in the regular classroom.

Look at the chart below. It summarizes some of the needs and concerns of gifted students along with suggested strategies and techniques that regular classroom teachers can use as tools to meet these needs. Other chapters of this book discuss many of these tools.

Needs and Concerns	Strategies and Techniques
1. Student already knows the skill or concept which is being taught.	1. Curriculum Compacting Learning Contract Collaboration with other teachers Use of technology
2. Student will learn the information, skills and/or concepts faster than most others in the class.	2. Independent study Become a class expert on some facet of the topic Thematic units Ability grouping
3. Student could become interested in the topic, but the teaching style does not match his learning style.	3. Individual Student Lesson Plan based on learning styles Multiple Intelligence Lesson Plan form
4. Student does not feel he/she is being academically or intellectually challenged.	4. Learning activities that focus on the higher levels of Bloom's Taxonomy Enrichment activities that involve real life problem solving Acceleration strategies
5. Student has given up on school, is unmotivated, wants to be entertained rather than work.	5. Pursuit of special interest area Personal interest and attention from one "special teacher" Personal goal setting Development of self confidence

CURRICULUM COMPACTING

Dr. Joseph Renzulli designed the process of Curriculum Compacting as a way of documenting mastery of the skills and content in the regular classroom while allowing the student more time to do acceleration and enrichment activities.

On the next page is a sample Compactor form. You will need one for each student who compacts a portion of the curriculum. Some suggested steps and guidelines for Curriculum Compacting are as follows:

- Begin with part of the regular curriculum that is easy to pretest. Decide what percentage of correct answers students will need in order to 'test out' of the regular classroom work. Any student, not just those identified as gifted, should have the opportunity to take the pretest.

- Use the Compactor to record the pretest score or any other evidence you have used to show mastery.

- The Skill, Content or Unit of Work section indicates the particular skill, concept, textbook chapter or unit the student has mastered.

- The Alternate Activities are those activities the student will work on while the rest of the class is doing grade level work. These can be from the same subject area or can involve the student's particular area of interest. Look at activities from an *Individual Student Lesson Plan* or from the Questivities™ found in this book for suggestions and ideas.

- Assess the Alternate Activities completed by the student by using some type of authentic assessment criteria (see Chapter 6), but the grade given for the subject area should be the grade on the pretest.

- Each student should keep a folder containing the Compactor form and all of the work done in the Alternate Activities.

- Alternate Activities should be student choice activities. Do not tell the student he or she must use the time to remediate an area of weakness. Compactor time is valuable time for gifted students to work at their own level and pace on something of interest to them!

- Set rules and guidelines for behavior and plan some of your time to work with Compactor students. Compactor time is not free time or play time!

- Check frequently on Compactor activities to offer suggestions and monitor progress.

- Working independently on a Compactor assignment is an excellent way for gifted students to develop organization and time management skills. However, they may need help in this area; do not assume they already know these skills!

CURRICULUM COMPACTOR FORM

Student's Name _____

Skill, Content or Unit of Work	Documentation of Mastery	Student Choice Alternate Activities

USING THE LEARNING CONTRACT

Another tool that works well with many gifted students is the Learning Contract. This allows for both acceleration and enrichment. Acceleration is studying material at a faster pace and a higher grade level than would normally be the case. Collaborating with another teacher at a higher grade level is one way to get information and materials to use in acceleration. Accelerated learning activities can be done within the regular classroom, by going to another classroom, with a mentor or other adult volunteer, or even by attending another school for a portion of the day.

Enrichment activities include studying areas of learning which are usually not included in the regular curriculum. Often this means delving into a subject more deeply than would otherwise be the case. Many student choice activities in the *Individual Student Lesson Plans* are appropriate as enrichment activities for gifted students.

The reproducible Learning Contract on the next page also includes space to write those activities that will be done with the rest of the class, and working conditions where behavior, project management, and time management strategies are enumerated. Use the Checkpoint dates to help students stay on task and lessen the chances of procrastination and last minute panic!

LEARNING CONTRACT for _____

Subject/Thematic Unit/Topic _____

Required activities to be done by the entire class:

Date	Activity	Date	Activity
____	_____	____	_____
____	_____	____	_____
____	_____	____	_____

Acceleration Options

Check your
choice(s)

____	_____	____	_____
____	_____	____	_____
____	_____	____	_____

Enrichment Options

Check your
choice(s)

____	_____	____	_____
____	_____	____	_____
____	_____	____	_____

Working Conditions

Rules/Terms of Contract　　　　　　　　　　　**Checkpoint Dates**

_____　　　　_____

_____　　　　_____

_____　　　　_____

_____　　　　_____

USING VARIOUS FORMS OF GROUPING AS EFFECTIVE TEACHING TOOLS WITH GIFTED STUDENTS

There has been much discussion and conflicting opinions in recent years about the best way to group gifted students in school. I believe that each of the various forms of grouping for teaching and learning is effective. Why throw away any of these forms? Instead, think of instructional groups as flexible, not permanent, and use them as circumstances dictate.

Homogeneous/Ability Grouping

This type of grouping clusters students of similar ability or interest. Use it for remediation, acceleration, and enrichment. One way to structure such groups is by multi-grade levels. Here the teacher groups students of similar ability or interests. Dr. Karen Rogers, an expert in ability grouping, supports its benefit for gifted students. Her research shows that almost any way of grouping gifted students together, full or part time, will produce substantial academic gains when compared to equally gifted children who are never grouped by ability. [9]

Heterogeneous Grouping

This type of grouping combines students of differing abilities or interests. It facilitates the learning of common objectives, and works best when reading levels or math proficiencies are not involved. It is good for group projects promoting creativity and can be used with cooperative learning, small group discussion, role playing, and affective curriculum.

Heterogeneous grouping provides gifted students with opportunities for peer tutoring, learning to work in teams, leadership development, and improves socialization and understanding between students. A word of caution. Use peer tutoring sparingly with gifted students. They should not spend the majority of their time in school tutoring others.

Gifted students often benefit when grouped heterogeneously by age and homogeneously by ability and/or interest area.

Individualized Instruction

This type of grouping facilitates the management of many achievement levels.

It involves self paced learning at each student's performance level, and can be used for remediation, enrichment, or acceleration. It is good to use in exploring each student's interest areas. Individualized instruction teaches independent learning and helps develop individual responsibility. It must be monitored and appropriately evaluated. (See the Learning Contract on the previous page as an example of how to implement this strategy.)

Whole Class Instruction

This "old fashioned" method is both efficient and effective when presenting new content that all need to know. It works well with many types of audiovisual presentations, for initial instruction and some enrichment activities. Teacher directed instruction is still very beneficial for all students, including the gifted.

DEVELOPING A PHILOSOPHY OF GIFTED EDUCATION

The Richardson Study, a national study on educating able learners conducted by the Sid W. Richardson Foundation from 1982-1985, recommended that school districts and communities develop a written philosophy for the education of able learners consistent with local goals and values. I have worked with several school districts throughout the United States to develop such philosophies. Below is a reproducible page you can use to begin writing your own philosophy of gifted education. Use it with other teachers, parents, and community leaders to develop a gifted philosophy in your school district. A sample philosophy combined from several I have helped to develop is on the next page. Use it as a model and a tool in developing your own.[10]

A PHILOSOPHY OF GIFTED EDUCATION

I believe that gifted students:

I believe that a program for gifted students:

SAMPLE PHILOSOPHY OF GIFTED EDUCATION

We believe that gifted students:

1. Have highly individualized needs reflected in high intellectual abilities, unique talents, and differences in learning styles, emotional needs, and social development.

2. Possess potential for independent and critical thinking and benefit from active exploration, questioning, and investigation.

3. Require continuous stimulation and encouragement in the areas of motivation and social interaction necessary to reach their maximum potential.

We believe that a program for gifted students:

1. Should meet the needs of gifted students K-12 by serving a variety of types of giftedness.

2. Should be differentiated to accommodate divergent thinking and higher level thinking skills.

3. Should provide in-depth enrichment in areas of student interest emphasizing research, communication, and study skills.

4. Should provide guidance and counseling services for emotional support and career education.

5. Should provide for community involvement through college classes, dual enrollment, mentor and external programs, resource professionals, etc.

6. Should be funded so that the program can have well-equipped instructional spaces comparable to regular classrooms with qualified instructors who meet with their classes on a regular basis.

7. Should provide a means of regular communication between the gifted and regular classroom teachers and between teachers and parents.

8. Should include the time spent in the regular classroom so that gifted students are not receiving an appropriate education only when they go to the "gifted class."

9. Should adequately challenge all gifted students.

10. Should involve teachers, parents and students in planning and implementation.

Developed by Carolyn Coil with several school districts throughout the United States.

Self Assessment: Meeting the Needs of Gifted and Talented Students

Teacher Reflection Page

1=Most of the time   2=Some of the time   3=Seldom   4=Almost never

The curriculum and learning activities in my classroom and/or school meet the needs of gifted and talented learners by:

_____ 1. Presenting content related to broad based themes.

_____ 2. Integrating several different subject areas.

_____ 3. Presenting comprehensive, related experiences within an area of study.

_____ 4. Allowing for student choices in studying an area of special interest.

_____ 5. Developing independent study skills.

_____ 6. Developing higher level thinking skills.

_____ 7. Focusing on open-ended tasks, questions and answers.

_____ 8. Developing advanced research skills, particularly in "real life" settings.

_____ 9. Integrating basic skills with critical and creative thinking skills.

_____ 10. Encouraging the development of new and unique ideas, materials, methods, techniques, products, performances or processes.

_____ 11. Providing opportunities for and guidance in the development of leadership skills.

_____ 12. Guiding students in the development of social skills, self confidence and self understanding.

_____ 13. Facilitating curriculum compacting, acceleration and enrichment.

_____ 14. Considering multiple intelligences and a variety of learning styles.

_____ 15. Providing for advanced study with a mentor, business partner or other resource person.

What are your areas of strength in differentiating curriculum for gifted and talented students? (Look at items rated 1 and 2)

What are your areas of weakness in differentiating curriculum for gifted and talented students? (Look at items rated 3 and 4)

Reflections

* Gifted students have outstanding abilities in academics, creativity, leadership and/or the arts. They differ in individual gifts and talents which makes the term gifted difficult to define.

* Gifted students need a differentiated curriculum that will challenge them to work hard and to achieve excellence.

* There are many inclusion strategies to use with gifted students in the regular classroom.

* Various forms of grouping gifted and talented students are effective depending on the circumstances and learning objectives.

* School districts and communities need to develop a written Philosophy of Gifted Education.

NOTES

[9] GSG Newsletter, Winter, 1993

[10] Cox, June, Neil Daniel & Bruce Boston, Educating Able Learners

Chapter 12

THE NATURE OF CONFLICT

Questons to Consider

1. Why is it important to learn how to prevent and manage conflict?

2. What are some of the causes of and outcomes resulting from conflict?

3. What strategies can we use to deal with conflict constructively?

4. What benefits can be derived from teaching students about conflict and conflict resolution?

It was Monday afternoon and the week had not started well. Mr. Marks, the Assistant Principal, had done nothing all day except deal with students who were in conflict with one another. Several groups of boys had gotten off the buses arguing and fighting, mostly about things that had happened in their neighborhoods over the weekend. Two boys were threatening to have a fight after school because a certain university team had lost a football game! Two girls were fighting over a boyfriend and another group of students was accusing each other of cheating on a test. It seemed to Mr. Marks that conflicts, potential violence, and hostility were everywhere.

Ms. Gomez and Ms. Dunn listened carefully when the principal explained that there needed to be much more collaboration among teachers during the upcoming school year. Each felt that they would be better off just closing their doors and teaching like they always had. After all, both had seen new ideas come and go. Furthermore, they felt resentful when they learned they were to collaborate with one another and share responsibility for each other's students. Like many other teachers, Ms. Gomez and Ms. Dunn felt some of the internal conflict change inevitably brings. Neither felt very positive about being part of a collaborative team.

Mr. Marks is not alone. While we strive for the goal of having a 'safe and orderly environment' in all our schools, the reality often is that teachers and principals spend a great deal of time just trying to prevent and manage conflicts. The reactions of Ms. Gomez and Ms. Dunn are typical, too. Conflict is invariably part of the change process. Most schools are involved in a variety of changes. Typically, some people want change while others wish to maintain the status quo. And even those who favor change may have different points of view. Conflict is inevitable.

For these reasons, the ability to prevent and manage conflicts is one of the major needs of schools today and into the 21st century. In this chapter, we will look at conflicts and the tools we can use to deal with them in the school setting.

Definition of Conflict

A **conflict** is a state of tension or disagreement between two or more people, ideas, nations, systems, or communities. It occurs as a byproduct of our interdependence on one another. People deal with conflict in different ways. Some are conflict avoiders and seek to deny or postpone conflict at all costs. At the other extreme are persons who are always looking for a fight or dispute. Most people fall somewhere between these two extremes.

Causes of Conflict

Several things may cause conflicts. Major causes are:

1. **Scarcity** (or perceived scarcity) of something that more than one person or group wants, such as goods, money, rewards, prizes, privileges, status, advancement, etc. Schools often are faced with conflicts due to scarcity. Students may feel that other students get more privileges or opportunities than they do. Parents complain that their child is not receiving equitable treatment or services. Teachers often feel that certain favored staff members get more than their fair share of scarce resources, citing everything from curricular materials to a duty free lunch. When there are many wants and needs and not enough resources or rewards, conflict will occur.

2. **Differences in values or opinions** within a given system, such as goals that should be worked for, the direction an organization should go, the rules or laws that should be made, etc. Differences in values and opinions have always been part of the American landscape. In fact, our Founding Fathers shaped our democracy with the knowledge that a free people would have diverse opinions. As our schools become less homogeneous and more culturally diverse, and as society as a whole has difficulty choosing a common set of values, these differences are going to cause conflicts in schools. Administrators, students, teachers, various groups of parents, political leaders and others will express conflicting opinions about the nature and role of the school. This will continue to be a source of conflict well into the 21st century.

3. **Pressure and emotions** experienced by individuals who cause "explosions" toward one another. Many people experience a great deal of stress and pressure. Usually, most people handle their stress well, but we all go through times when we have more than enough! When pressures mount and emotions boil over, conflict can result. When this happens, the conflict at hand is usually not the underlying problem. It is more likely to be the symptom of other problems.

4. **Personality factors** that are a part of each person that surface when facing the anxieties and problems of life. Some people take an aggressive, unyielding stance when faced with conflict or disagreement. Others are not assertive and expect that others will somehow read their minds. These people get hurt when they discover their needs have not been met. Some people approach conflict with no emotion, others are excessively emotional. These different personalities add to the complexity of conflict resolution.

Conflict: Positive or Negative?

Conflict can have both positive and negative outcomes. Whether the conflict has a positive or negative influence on those involved depends largely upon how the participants handle the conflict. Does it escalate to the point it becomes violent and unmanageable resulting in destruction? Or are the dynamics of the situation managed to promote growth and new directions for the participants? Either outcome is possible from a conflict situation.

Positive Outcomes from Conflict Situations

1. Provides drama and adventure.

2. Gives an opportunity to explore differences and hear both sides.

3. Motivates people to engage in problem solving and change the situation.

4. Clears the air and provides both parties with a better understanding of one another.

5. Improves communication and creates new perspectives.

6. Contributes to long term wellness if the conflict is resolved.

7. Can be a catalyst for energy and creativity.

Negative Outcomes from Conflict Situations

1. Can cause hurt feelings.

2. Increases anger that can lead to threats, violence, and destruction.

3. Causes emotional and/or communication breakdowns.

4. Person who doesn't like conflict will withdraw and the problem isn't solved.

5. Leads to illnesses caused by stress.

6. May be costly in terms of time, money and other resources.

7. May result in physical harm or death.

8. Takes emphasis off other things that are more important. For example, settling fights instead of academic learning; bickering rather than collaborating.

Conflict Management and Conflict Resolution

People involved in conflicts can manage them effectively if they learn to trust the other person(s) involved and not let the negative tension that comes from conflict engulf them. Use the 10 steps listed below as guidelines in resolving and managing the conflicts you face.

10 Steps to Successful Conflict Resolution

1. Establish the appropriate physical environment and personal attitude. Build rapport and avoid blaming the other person.

2. Make sure everyone agrees on what the conflict is really about. Stick to the problem at hand. Do not let personal issues get in the way of conflict resolution.

3. Talk about needs, feelings, and interests instead of opinions or positions of disagreement. Try to see the other person's point of view as well as your own.

4. Restate the issues in the conflict so that it is possible to find common ground. Focusing on common problems, interests or goals often lead to common solutions and areas of agreement.

5. Work on the easiest areas for resolution, the part that seems most likely to be solved, first.

6. Brainstorm possible solutions that address the needs of both sides. Use objective criteria when exploring possible solutions.

7. Have acceptable alternatives in mind to suggest if you don't get exactly what you want.

8. Collaborate on an equitable solution. Try to come to agreement on a joint action that is acceptable to all involved.

9. Accommodate face saving for all parties

10. Communicate, communicate, communicate! This is the best tool for resolving any conflict.

CONFLICT IN THE PRIMARY GRADES

Prevention

Prevention is the KEY in avoiding conflicts among children in the classroom. It is possible to set up your classroom so that, for the most part, conflict will not occur. Structure the day so that there is a combination of quiet and active activities. Make one of the rules of the class "Be kind to others." This covers a multitude of behaviors including any situation that might involve conflict. Go over the rules every day and use the rule whenever a potential conflict arises. The teacher must constantly MODEL the "Be kind to others" rule and point out to the students when being kind. If the teacher models and reinforces good behavior, it will happen. Before breaking into small groups for any activity with movement or any type of give and take among children, discuss limits, classroom rules and sharing.

Most conflict in the early grades has to do with learning to share and taking turns. Watch for children who are doing these things and give them positive feedback. Praise students when they are doing something that follows the rule of being kind. Some primary aged children can be talked to at their chronological age level, but others have the social development of two or three year olds, and their reasoning skills may not yet be developed. The teacher must consider developmental age, not chronological age, when dealing with conflicts among young children. Meet them where they are and bring them forward.

Resolving Classroom Conflicts

As much as possible, allow the students to resolve their own problems. Point out and define the problem for your students and then help them in learning how to resolve the situation. Remove both parties from the group for a specified amount of time if participants cannot resolve a classroom conflict.

Use direct intervention if physical harm could come to a student as a result of the conflict situation.

CONFLICT AND OLDER STUDENTS

Prevention

The key to avoiding conflicts is prevention. At the beginning of the school year when you review the class rules, include rules that will reduce the possibility of conflicts developing in your classroom. Often, verbal taunts and accusations lead to greater conflicts among students. Therefore, some of your rules should be guidelines for verbal exchanges between students. Often your students can collaborate with you in making classroom rules that result in fewer situations of conflict. State these rules and guidelines in a positive way. Some examples, which were all developed with the help of students, are:

- ✓ Use words that will build others up when talking to or about them.
- ✓ Talk in a positive way when you have comments to make about others.
- ✓ If something is bothering you about another person, talk to that person directly about the problem. Ask for help in solving the problem rather than making accusations.
- ✓ Give compliments, not criticisms, to others.

Conflict

Teacher Reflection Page

Think about the conflicts you have faced in the last few months. Review the information found on the previous pages to help you reflect on these questions.

1. Think about a conflict that you have had with another staff member at your school. Consider the following issues:

- What was the major cause of the conflict?
- Did both parties agree on what the conflict was really about?
- Was the conflict resolved to your satisfaction?
- What were some unspoken issues in this conflict?
- Was trust and rapport present?
- Was one person in a more powerful negotiating position?
- How did this affect the outcome or resolution of the conflict?
- What were the positive outcomes of the conflict? Negative outcomes?
- What would you do differently if a similar situation occurs again?

2. Consider a conflict you have had with a parent. Think about the following:

- What common goals and interests did you and the parent have?
- What emotional or personal attitudes made it difficult to resolve this conflict?
- What alternatives did you offer that would meet the needs of both persons?
- Would it have been helpful to have involved more people? Fewer people? Why?
- In which areas was there good communication?
- In which areas did communication tend to break down?

3. List several conflicts involving students. Choose one and then consider

- What was the cause of the conflict?
- What positive outcomes occurred?
- What negative outcomes occurred?
- What strategies did you use in solving the conflict?
- What other strategies could you have used?

4. What are some of your strengths in resolving or managing conflicts? What are some of your weaknesses?

5. What would you like to change about your conflict management style and strategies?

Rivalries Between Students

Beginning in the intermediate grades and through adolescence, rivalries between groups of students seem to develop quickly. These begin with one child deciding she/he does not like another. He or she then tries to pull others to his or her side. This type of situation can escalate quickly. If you are aware this is taking place, action on your part can squelch the conflict almost immediately. Take these steps:

☐ Gather all involved.

☐ Ask each person to tell his/her version of what is going on.

☐ When one person is talking, no one is to interrupt.

☐ Analyze the underlying causes of the conflict.

☐ Mentally pinpoint ringleaders.

☐ Verbalize the situation as you see it.

☐ Make a suggestion of what you would do.

☐ Ask for other suggestions to help solve the problem.

☐ Come to consensus.

When you lead students through this problem solving method, verbalize to them the reason you are guiding them is because you care about all of them and you are concerned. A level of trust between teacher and students needs to be present for this method to work successfully.

CONFLICTS AND VIOLENCE ON THE OUTSIDE

Many students come to school with "little storm clouds" hanging over their heads. They bring to school the troubles and problems they face during the 18 hours of the day when they are not in school. They often struggle with a negative attitude that they bring into the classroom from their homes or neighborhoods. If you are a good listener, you can often gain a great deal of information about what is going on outside school. Conflicts that begin in the neighborhood or on the bus sometimes escalate during the school day. Other disagreements that start at school continue as the students go home in the afternoon. When you become aware this is happening, talk it over with the students involved.

Parents and Conflict

Keep a record of specific behaviors and situations for each child. If this type of attitude continues in spite of teacher interventions and problem solving, call the parents. Parents sometimes deny that there is conflict at home. Even when we as teachers know that this is not so, our position is not to fix their home. We can only deal with what is happening at school. What we're teaching students about getting along with others and about correct behavior and relationships with others may be directly opposite of what they experience at home. So the home and the school send mixed messages. Our values in the school are not necessarily the same values the parents have. Consider these scenarios.

Some students were using bad language. When the teacher remarked, "We don't use ugly words when we talk to one another," one student replied, "My mama says those words hundreds of times every day."

One student was seen hitting another student. When the teacher said, "We don't hit other people," this boy responded, "I hit my Dad sometimes. My Dad hits my Mom, and he hits me, so I hit him back."

As these two examples illustrate, violence and conflict in both word and deed are commonplace in some homes. For some of our students, this is considered the behavioral norm. When confronted by such attitudes teachers need to show students there is another way to manage conflicts. This does not mean pointing out to students why and how their parents are wrong. It does mean showing by example in the classroom and school setting how to resolve conflicts without violence. This includes using active listening skills and problem solving skills so that all points of view are heard and a number of options for resolving the conflict are considered.

Conflict in our Culture

Remember that conflict often results from a difference in values and opinions. The values we teach in school about managing conflict in nonviolent ways is a very different message from the messages given to children in the pop culture, on television, videos, and computer games, on the streets, and sometimes in their own homes.

The students were loud as they filed into first period class on the day after the shooting. Television crews were all over town, and it seemed that the killing of a tourist was big news. One student said to his teacher, "My uncle was killed last month, and I didn't see no television cameras here then. He and this other guy was fighting over something and the gun went off and he was dead."

In 1994 and 1995, news reports focused on violent incidents involving foreign tourists in Florida. While the news media publicized the murders of these tourists, many more "local" Floridians were being shot and killed on a daily basis. Reports of these killings never made it to the national news, but local news organizations took note. The kids were very aware of this local violence, and for many, their role model was one of solving conflict in a violent way.

One way to deal with student attitudes about conflict and conflict among students themselves is to include lessons about conflict in your ongoing curriculum. Some tools for doing this can be found on the next few pages. Begin with the *Student Questionnaire.* This will give you and your students insights about how they personally react in situations of conflict with a variety of people. This is a good activity to use in helping students discover the personal nature of conflict. Their reactions to situations most often depend upon who the conflict is with.

You will find a *Lesson Plan for Conflict Management* that focuses students on the concept of conflict in a less personal way. There are also a sample thematic unit, Lesson Planning Format, and Questivities™ to use in a more in-depth study of **Conflict.**

Reflections:

* The ability to prevent and manage conflict is a major need for anyone who interacts with others in some way.

* Conflict has many causes and can have both positive and negative outcomes.

* Prevention, problem solving and direct intervention are three strategies for dealing with conflicts between students.

* Lessons about conflict and conflict resolution can help students learn to handle conflicts effectively.

Notes

STUDENT QUESTIONNAIRE

Name _____ . . . . Grade _____

When you have a conflict or a disagreement with someone, how do you react? You may react differently depending upon the person. Listed below you will find several types of people you live, work and play with.

For each of these people, complete the sentence: "When I disagree with or have a conflict with this person, I usually..."

1. Parent:

2. Brother or sister:

3. Step-parent:

4. Grandparent:

5. Teacher:

6. Classmate I don't like:

7. Person who has called me names:

8. Someone of a different racial or ethnic group:

9. Someone who hangs around in a different crowd than I do:

10. My best friend:

Conflict Management Lesson Plan

1. Definition

On newsprint or the chalkboard, write the word CONFLICT. Ask the students what they think it means. Write their definitions.

2. Compare and contrast the Shades of Meaning

Compare and contrast the definitions the students have generated plus any of your own that have not been mentioned. Discuss similarities and differences in the meanings.

3. Making a Continuum

Draw a horizontal line the full length of the chalkboard. Write *Less Severe* at the end of the line to the left and *Most Severe* at the end of the line on the right. Divide the students into small groups. Ask each group to write each of the definitions where they think they should be placed on the continuum. Discuss the placements, having students from the different groups write the placement on the chalkboard.

4. Categorizing Types of Conflict

Write each of these phrases on a piece of newsprint or overhead transparency:

Conflict within yourself

Conflict between groups of people in the same family/school/ neighborhood/town/state/country

Conflict between countries

Conflict between ideas

Assign each small group a type of conflict. Have each group prepare and then perform a skit illustrating their type of conflict.

5. Discussion

Are conflicts ever worth having?

When are they detrimental?

When are they helpful?

From ***Motivating Underachievers*** by Carolyn Coil. Pieces of Learning. Beavercreek OH

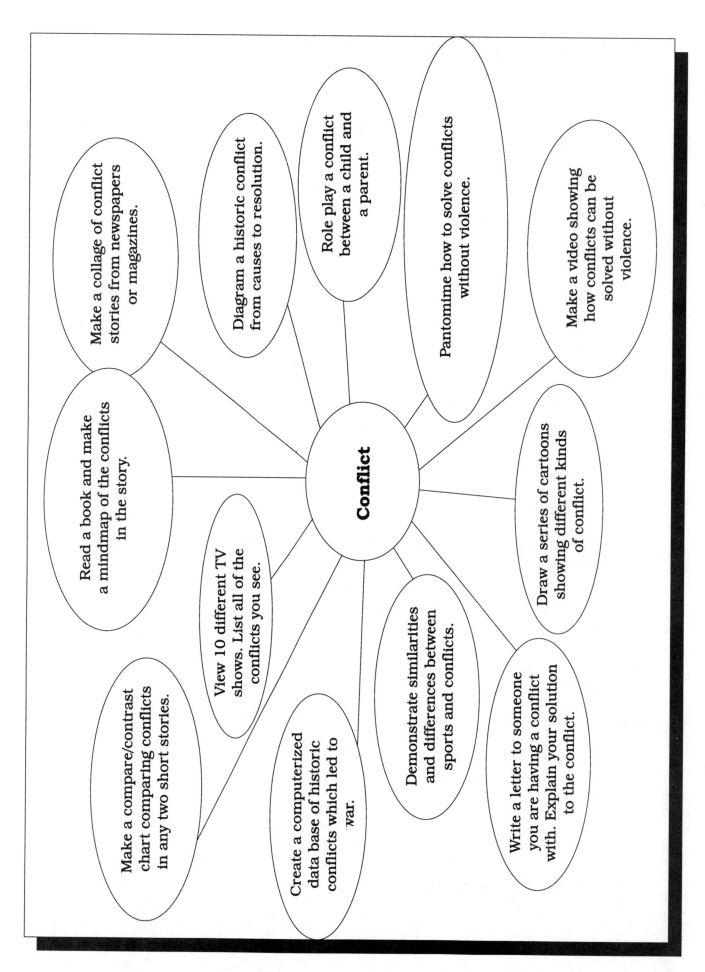

The central concept is **Conflict**, surrounded by the following activities:

- Make a collage of conflict stories from newspapers or magazines.
- Diagram a historic conflict from causes to resolution.
- Role play a conflict between a child and a parent.
- Pantomime how to solve conflicts without violence.
- Make a video showing how conflicts can be solved without violence.
- Read a book and make a mindmap of the conflicts in the story.
- Make a compare/contrast chart comparing conflicts in any two short stories.
- View 10 different TV shows. List all of the conflicts you see.
- Create a computerized data base of historic conflicts which led to war.
- Demonstrate similarities and differences between sports and conflicts.
- Write a letter to someone you are having a conflict with. Explain your solution to the conflict.
- Draw a series of cartoons showing different kinds of conflict.

INDIVIDUAL LESSON PLAN - LEARNING MODALITIES

ACTIVITIES - STUDENT CHOICES

Visual

1. Make a compare/contrast chart comparing conflicts in any two short stories.
2. Diagram a historic conflict from causes to resolution.
3. Draw a series of cartoons showing different kinds of conflict.

Verbal

7. Read a book and make a mindmap of the conflicts in the story.
8. Role play a conflict between a child and a parent.
9. Write a letter to someone you are having a conflict with. Explain your solution to the conflict.

Kinesthetic

4. Make a collage of conflict stories from newspapers or magazines.
5. Pantomime how to solve conflicts without violence.
6. Demonstrate similarities and differences between sports and conflicts.

Technological

10. View 10 different TV shows. List all of the conflicts you see.
11. Make a video showing how conflicts can be solved without violence.
12. Create a computerized data base of historic conflicts which led to war.

Required Activities Teacher's Choice

1. Generate a list of class rules & procedures that will help prevent conflicts.
2. Use a problem solving method to identify & solve an existing classroom conflict.
3. Do Conflict Managements Lesson.

Product/Performance Required

1. Class list of rules and procedures.
2. Mutually agreed upon solution.
3. Continuum of conflicts

Assessment Required Activities

1. List agreed upon by all class members; group participation
2. Problem was identified; criteria generated and used in problem solving
3. Logical reasons for placement of types of conflicts on continuum.

Optional Student-Parent Cooperative Activity

Using a problem solving method to identify and solve an existing conflict between student and parent.

Product/Performance Student Choice

Assessment Student Choice

Student Choices in Ways to Learn

Visual

_____
_____

Kinesthetic

_____
_____

Verbal

_____
_____

Technological

_____
_____

Conflict

Learning Modality
Verbal

Learning Style
Abstract Random

Taxonomy Level
Application

Multiple Intelligence
Verbal/Linguistic
Interpersonal

> Role play a conflict between two students or between a child and a parent. Make sure the conflict comes to some resolution.

Assessment
1. Clarity of conflict
2. Resolution of conflict
3. Flow of presentation
4. Preparation

Project Question
What would a typical conflict be between two students
Or between children and parents?

Questivities
List typical conflicts between students or between children and parents.
Compare/contrast a conflict with a parent and a conflict with another student.
Would you rather avoid a conflict or resolve the problem even though it would cause an argument?
How would you feel if you had an opinion about a controversial issue and all of your Friends had the opposite opinion?
Why are so many conflicts settled with violence?
How can conflicts be resolved so that both sides are satisfied?
What would happen if conflicts in school were never resolved?
If there were no conflicts in your school?

Active Questioning
Make a list of questions your mom or dad might ask you about an issue you disagree about.

Chapter 13

Parent/Teacher Collaboration

Questions to Consider

1. What are the essential skills in communicating with parents?

2. Why are trust and respect so important in building collaborative relationships?

3. What are the purposes of Parent-Teacher conferences?

4. How can teachers develop effective strategies to involve parents?

Ms. Fenwick breathed a sigh of relief. Her students were gone for the day and she could take a moment to relax. She smiled as she thought about the exuberance of the six and seven year olds she teaches every day. She tried to remember her own childhood and thought back to her own first grade class. "The thing I remember most," she decided, "was trying to write the letters of the alphabet so that each looked perfect on my paper. I would get so frustrated when my attempts didn't look as good as the teacher's examples! I don't know if any of my students even care about things like that."

Growing up in a world that is welcoming the 21st century isn't the same as growing up in the 1950's, 1960's, 1970's or even the 1980's. Close your eyes and take a few moments to reflect on some memories from your own childhood. Then in the chart on the next page in the left-hand column, list the more outstanding things, events, places and activities you can remember. Next, in the right-hand column, list typical events, places and activities an average child in your class might experience today. As you look at the two lists, what conclusions can you make? What things have changed?

Memories from My Childhood	Typical Activities of Children Today

Observations:

Changes:

Conclusions:

Like teachers, parents are also feeling the effects of these tremendous changes. Parents look at everything going on in the world, in their community, and even within the school and may see vast differences from their childhood experiences. Often this is a good way to begin establishing a collaborative relationship with parents, for many parents and teachers look at the world through similar generational eyes.

If you are 15 or more years older or younger than the parents of your students, talk about differences between your childhood memories and theirs, and then reflect on further differences in their child's experiences.

"Collaboration" is one of the buzz words in education, but we must go further than merely repeating the appropriate words. We must sincerely want parent participation and input into their child's education. Parents need to be involved in the day-in and day-out activities of the school. The more they are involved, the more they will understand about the world their child lives in for a good portion of each day. The more parents are involved, the more they will appreciate, understand and support the schools.

Parents can provide valuable information about their child's behavior, educational concerns, strengths, weaknesses and how to manage the child. Additionally, recent research has shown that parental attitude and encouragement can affect school success at least as much as a child's IQ. Often the difference between children who do well in school and those who do not relates to their parents' attitudes about school. In other words, parental involvement enables children to achieve better and learn more.

Productive Communication between Parents and Teachers

The essentials in any productive communication involve skills in both talking and listening.

As good talkers, teachers must be sure that they express their ideas and concerns clearly and that parents understand them. State problems as simply as possible, and do not ignore or avoid them. It is very important for parents to understand when there are problems and why the problems are occurring. Therefore, it is essential to state a child's behavior in real terms that parents can understand and identify with. Be specific. Don't use educational jargon and say, *"We're seeing some signs of aggression in Jeremy."* Instead, explain the problem: *"Jeremy has been in three fights during recess this week."*

As good listeners, teachers must be sure they listen so they will really understand the parents' point of view. Concentrate on what the other person is saying. Don't be thinking about the next statement you will make and miss what the parent is saying. Too often what passes for listening is arguing mentally as the other person makes his or her points!

People often communicate more nonverbally than they do verbally. Be aware of the parent's nonverbal language and also what he or she is saying in words. Also be aware that different cultures have different types of nonverbal communication and customs. Eye contact or specific gestures may mean one thing to you and something completely different to a parent from a different ethnic background.

Cultural Characteristics Which May Affect Parent/Teacher Communication

African American
- Personal questions at first meeting may be seen as intrusive
- Verbally inventive with semantic inversions ("bad" may mean "good")
- Indirect eye contact when listening; direct eye contact when speaking
- Emotional intensity and expression during conversation
- Physically expressive with gestures and body language
- Deep sense of cultural history

Hispanic
- Physical closeness during conversation (12 to 18 inches apart)
- Flexible sense of time
- Extended family important
- Hissing to get attention is acceptable
- Sustained direct eye contact may be interpreted as a challenge to authority
- Eye contact is important during conversation
- Emotional intensity in conversation

Asian American
- Reserved with a respect for silence and control
- Orientation toward privacy with disdain for public reprimand
- Drop eyes to show respect
- Laugh when embarrassed (particularly true for females)
- May take offense at the use of nicknames or first names only
- May be considered inappropriate to shake hands with a person of the opposite sex
- Parent/teacher conference may be regarded as a meeting where bad news will be given

Anglo American
- Value direct and polite conversation
- Nuclear family more important than extended family
- Preference for promptness
- Emotional restraint in public behavior
- Competitive and individualistic
- May want comparisons of own child to others in class

Key Elements of Good Communication

Teacher Reflection Page

Take a few minutes to jot down what you feel are the key elements of good speaking and of good listening. Then discuss your ideas with several other teachers. As a group list these elements and share this information at a staff meeting.

List 5 important elements of good listening:

1.

2.

3.

4.

5.

List 5 important elements of good speaking:

1.

2.

3.

4.

5.

Developing Trust and Respect Between School and Home

Many teachers look upon the idea of parent/teacher collaboration as a source of stress and anxiety. Teachers may be reluctant to share information about a student or may be afraid of criticism or of not living up to parental expectations.

Parents also may be reluctant to enter into a collaborative relationship with the school. They may have negative attitudes toward teachers based on their own childhood school experiences. They may have had unpleasant experiences with teachers and other school personnel previously when they were trying to help their child. Negative feelings may also stem from problems they have had with their child, feelings of failure, or feel blamed or guilty for something that has gone wrong at home or school.

The critical factors of trust and rapport are repeatedly the most important things in a parent-teacher relationship. Parents can see the same issues in either a positive or a negative way. It is the trust factor that makes the difference.

Things for Teachers to Remember About Parents

There may be several causes for parents' behaviors and attitudes toward you. Consider the following factors when you wonder why parents are acting in a certain way:

✓ Their childhood experiences

✓ Their experiences with teachers and schools
✓ Their relationships with their parents
✓ Their fears and insecurities
✓ Their hopes and expectations
✓ Their careers and work
✓ Their relationship with their spouse
✓ Their self confidence or lack of it
✓ Their current emotional status
✓ Their experiences with other children and the school

An essential element in building an atmosphere conducive to effective parent/teacher collaboration is having a *Circle of Respect* that involves students, parents and their teachers. This means that all parties truly respect and trust one another. They have the confidence that each is doing his or her best to work toward excellence in the learning process. A break anywhere in this circle usually results in a breakdown in student performance.

Unfortunately, teachers, parents and students do not always promote this sense of mutual respect. Do your best to keep the *Circle of Respect* intact at your school. If it is broken, see what you can do to rebuild the mutual respect of all those in your school who are involved in the education of children.

Planning the Parent/Teacher Conference

One way to establish a collaborative relationship with parents is through the Parent/Teacher Conference. This provides a structured opportunity for parents and teachers to discuss mutual concerns and to work together. Successful Parent/

Teacher Conferences require planning. Part of this planning is to realize that sometimes participants may come to the conference with hidden agendas. It is important to consider this before planning the conference itself.

Hidden agendas and fears often break the *Circle of Respect*. Either a parent or a teacher may come to the conference with a hidden agenda. These agendas exist for many reasons. Sometimes people don't understand their own feelings very well, or they may be embarrassed to admit how they really feel. There may be pressure from a third party or situation. Any of these factors may create hidden agendas. Some hidden agendas that may be present in the parent-teacher conference are:

• Need to assert power and control

• Need to feel needed

• Desire to impress the others at the conference

• Protection of a loved one

• Feelings of inadequacy

• Need to appease the other parent, especially if that parent is not at the conference

• Desire for help or intervention but not knowing how to ask

• Need to impress colleagues or superiors

• Negative feelings about a certain group or a certain type of parents/teachers

Providing a structure and using it to plan ahead of time are important in parent/teacher conferences. Because the input of parents and collaboration between parents and teachers is so valuable, teachers need to approach the conference in a way that ensures that the greatest benefit can be derived from it.

One way to do this is to plan thoroughly for the conference, using a checklist of important points. This structure enables teachers to review the items that need to be prepared, spot check for good communication during the conference, and schedule follow-up details after the conference is over. This structure gives a concrete way to make sure you are really doing what your good intentions want to do in the first place!

The ***Parent/Teacher Conference Checklist*** provides a structure for conferences and simplifies all of the little details that are often overlooked because of a teacher's busy schedule. Use this tool as you plan your Parent/Teacher Conferences.

How to Gather Relevant Documentation

There are a number of different ways to document student behavior and parent contacts. Here are some suggestions:

✓ Use a small notebook using one page for each student.
✓ Keep a file of index cards with one card for each student.
✓ Utilize a folder that allows you to insert as many pages as are needed for each student as well as work samples.
✓ Devise a standard form for all phone contacts and conferences that can be used for all students.

Parent/Teacher Conference Checklist

Pre-Conference Planning

☐ 1. Verify meeting place, time and length, making sure this is convenient for the parent.

☐ 2. Communicate conference purpose.

        Purposes may include:
        Reporting on specific academic, behavioral or affective
        Strengths/weaknesses
        Information gathering
        Program planning
        Problem solving

☐ 3. Be familiar with the child.

        Study information in the child's file
        Know relevant data about tests, health, strengths, weaknesses, classwork
        Obtain information from other teachers as appropriate
        Gather work samples and other documentation
        Make sure you include positive aspects of a child's performance

☐ 4. Plan agenda.
        List conference purpose
        List items of concern to you
        Leave space to add parent concerns to the agenda

☐ 5. Arrange the physical environment.
        Privacy
        No distractions
        Comfortable temperature
        Seating arrangements
            No physical barriers between participants
            All participants should have a seat which indicates equal power
            Circular or square arrangement work best
            Use adult-sized chairs if possible - if parents must sit in small chairs, teacher should do the same
        Materials and work samples

The Conference

☐ 1. Welcome the parent.

    Greet the parent at the school office when possible.
    Be on time and have a contingency plan for emergency delays.
    Establish rapport through friendly comments and positive non-verbals.

☐ 2. Introduce agenda, purpose and conference timetable.

    Allow for parent additions.
    Give option for notetaking.

☐ 3. Listen and share information.

    Restate the purpose of the conference.
    Follow agenda, giving time for parent input at every stage.
    Communicate specific information.
    Stick to the issues.
    Ask for questions.

☐ 4. Summarize conference content and decisions.

☐ 5. Set dates and/or sequence of events for follow-up.

☐ 6. End in a positive way.

Post-Conference

☐ 1. Document and file conference agenda and notes.

☐ 2. Prepare a conference summary for parents.

☐ 3. Review with the child if appropriate.

☐ 4. Share information with other school personnel if appropriate.

      Note: Don't turn this into gossip about the child or the parent.
      What is said in the conference is not appropriate for staff room talk.

☐ 5. Establish time line for implementing conference follow-up.

☐ 6. Mark calendar and/or plan book for doing follow-up.

☐ 7. Complete any other documentation required by your school or district.

Be aware that parents are entitled to see any documentation in their child's cumulative record folder that goes from one grade to the next. According to the **Family Educational Rights and Privacy Act of 1974 (PL 93-380)** *parents have "the right to inspect and review any and all official records, files, and data directly related to their children, including all material that is incorporated into each student's cumulative record folder...specifically including, but not necessarily limited to, identifying data, academic work completed, level of achievement, attendance data, scores on standardized intelligence, aptitude and psychological tests, interest inventory results, health data, family background information, teacher or counselor ratings and observations, and verified reports of serious or recurrent behavior patterns."* [11]

Complexity of Parenting

Not only has family structure changed during the past 30 years, but also the skills needed to meet the demands placed on parents have grown more and more complex. Parents must fill numerous roles with their children and must do this while they are balancing a multitude of other demands. Many parents are simply overwhelmed at the task that confronts them. Some have all but given up.

Parents legitimately want to have a voice in the education of their children. When teachers and parents view the educational process as a collaborative effort, the parent-teacher conference becomes a key instructional strategy that enhances the child's growth and promotes more effective learning.

Other Ways to Communicate With Parents

Because teachers are so busy, good *intentions* about collaborating with parents are not enough. It simply will not happen unless you schedule it. Be sure to make a time for this to happen! Choose any of the following methods to communicate with the parents of your students.

1. Make positive phone calls to parents.

This is one of the most effective techniques. A brief update on the student is all that is needed. If a habit of positive phone calls is established, the lines of communication will be open when there is a problem. In a positive phone call:

- Describe the student's positive behavior

- Describe how you feel about the behavior

- Ask the parent to share what you have said with their child

A word of warning — If at all possible, don't make the first contact you have with the parent be a negative one!

2. Send notes, cards and letters to parents.

A positive note consists of a few lines written to the parent that tell something good about their child. Keep a file of ready-to-use notes. Plan to send home a specific number each week. Send preprinted messages, memos, and academic awards. Send home a birthday card on each student's birthday. Get well cards are important when a student is sick for more than a few days. Be sure to acknowledge parent help with a thank you note.

3. Use all types of home/school communication techniques.

Have students keep a daily journal which goes back and forth between home and school. Send student work home each Friday in a special envelope for parents.

Send home a weekly newsletter telling about events in your classroom and areas of study. Publicize school activities in the local newspaper.

4. Use new technologies.

Voice mail, E-mail, faxes, videos of student work, teleconferencing, World Wide Web pages, and other new technologies are helpful tools in communicating with parents. The Information Age can also be called the Communication Age. Take advantage of it!

Parents and Homework

Homework has the potential to be the most consistent day-to-day contact you have with parents, particularly in the upper grades. Yet parents complain that this is the greatest cause of conflict between them and their children. On the other hand, teachers complain that students don't complete assignments and parents won't see that they do. Often, parents don't understand why homework is given, when it will be given, how it is expected to be done, or what they can do to help.

Make sure you have a homework policy that states the expectations of students, parents and the teacher. Parents need to be kept informed about classwork, upcoming tests and projects, and ways they can help their child to study. Provide parents with suggestions for helping with homework and information about helping their child develop good study skills. **Becoming an Achiever** (Pieces of Learning, 1994) offers many such suggestions.

Parent Involvement

Parental involvement in schools usually begins with principals and teachers reaching out to parents and other family members. In many parts of the country, community and school leaders are collaborating to help meet the varied needs of today's students and their families. Each school and each teacher seem to discover the best ways for working with the parents of their students. Below are several suggestions you may want to consider as you develop effective strategies to involve parents in the educational process.

1. Encourage parents to complete one of the *Student Choice Learning Activities* from the *Individual Student Lesson Plan* format with their child. These should be learning activities and projects that will involve parents with their children in an enjoyable and creative way.

2. Distribute the reproducible *Message to Parents* to individual parents or to parent groups. Use it at parent meetings, parent/teacher conferences, and as an article in class or school newsletters. It can be a guide to assist you in discussing ways parents can help their children in many aspects of life.

3. Pay attention to environment, format, scheduling, child care, transportation, meals, and high visibility in the community when planning parental involvement programs.

4. Choose from 133 practical strategies in the book **"Involving Parents in Schools"** such as [12]

30. Take charge of a bulletin board in the hallway. This is your chance to present a positive message to every person that passes.

82. Bring a smile to a teacher's face by sending a bouquet of flowers during the week of parent-teacher conferences. The teacher, students, and every parent will enjoy the perky blooms.

A Message to Parents . . .

From Carolyn Coil

Parenting is a tough job as we welcome the 21st century. As parents, we try to do our best for our children, yet we often receive a variety of contradictory messages from the school, our friends and neighbors, our relatives, and the culture in general about what we should do to be "good parents" so that our children will "turn out okay."

All children need parental guidance and understanding. They need parents who will be advocates for their education. They need supporters to find resources for their intellectual and emotional growth. Many need assistance in developing organizational and study skills, in goal setting, in decision making, and in motivation. All of these are gifts that you can give to your children.

Guidance and Understanding

Think back to what life was like for you when you were the age your children are now. If you can remember some of the concerns and struggles you had at that time, you've taken a first step in developing a true understanding of your children.

Some of the inward elements of childhood and adolescence don't change very much from generation to generation; however, much in our world has changed drastically in the past 30 years. The problems and experiences our children have today are vastly different from a generation ago. Because of this, it takes more than looking back on the "good old days" to really understand the world our children inhabit.

Take time to be with your children. This is a simple statement, but it is difficult to do. Most parents have a multitude of work and household responsibilities which must somehow be juggled. Nevertheless, the gift of your own time is one of the greatest gifts you can give. Start by prioritizing your own life and find the time to be with your children.

Go to their activities. Be there when they bring friends home from school. Listen to their favorite music and find out what messages they are hearing in it. Know the television shows and videos they are watching, and take some time to watch with them. If you have a home computer that connects to the Internet, monitor your children's usage. There is a world of information at their fingertips, but there is a great deal of "rubbish" too!

Be aware of how much time they are spending on the computer, in front of the TV, or on the phone. Don't be afraid to comment on things you don't agree with, but be ready to listen to their point of view and get a dialogue going. Find out something about your child's interests, even if it's just enough to carry on a conversation about them. All of this will help you to develop a better understanding of your child and the world he or she lives in.

Give guidance to your child by discussing your values and morals and how you came to believe the way you do. There are such contradictory messages in the popular culture and within children's peer groups. Your views, even if they don't agree with them fully, will give your child a sense of security and point him toward a direction to travel as he goes through the journey of life.

. . . A Message to Parents

Resources for Intellectual and Emotional Growth

Keeping up with your child's needs in terms of schoolwork and leisure time activities can be a challenging undertaking. But this is one of the most important things you can do. Know what is going on in your child's classes at school. Be a strong advocate and partner in helping the school provide an appropriate education for your child and for all children.

Encourage your child to spend time in daily reading or study, even if no work has been specifically assigned. The development of good study skills and good organizational and time management skills does not come without practice. Establish a study hour in your home where study is done every night regardless of whether homework has been given.

Of course not all learning takes place inside the schoolhouse door or within the school curriculum. Children need access to a multitude of other resources and experiences to help them develop their talents fully. Find out what resources are available in your community. Theaters and art centers, libraries and bookstores, museums and state parks, historic buildings and wildlife preserves, ethnic villages and settlements are obvious places to start.

But some of the best community resources are not always the most obvious ones. A person in a nearby retirement home may be an expert in your child's area of special interest. A local radio station may have access to information which may fascinate your child. An ethnic restaurant may provide a window on a part of the world your child knows nothing about. Participating in a volunteer project may help develop many of the social skills your child needs. Look into such resources and encourage your children to take advantage of them as their needs and time allow.

The emotional needs of children are at least as important as their intellectual growth. Watch for signs of stress, particularly in children who are overloaded with activities or who tend to be perfectionists. The best thing to do for a stressed out child may simply be to make that child slow down, eliminate some activities, and relax. For a perfectionist, sharing stories of your own failures may help to show that experiencing failure is not the end of the world. In fact, you may be able to explain how one of your failures was actually a great learning experience in the long run.

Encourage motivation by being excited and enthusiastic about learning new things yourself, and share these with your children. Encourage self-confidence by pointing out not only your child's strengths and abilities, but also the efforts made in overcoming difficulties. Sometimes this effort leads to the greatest strengths of all. Help guide decision making, but allow your children to make their own decisions, and yes, sometimes their own mistakes, as that is how they learn and grow.

Children come with no guarantees. Nevertheless, parents can help them grow into adulthood well, each realizing their individual potential and becoming the adults they were meant to be.

NOTES

114. Be a resource finder. When browsing through bookstores examine the new children's books and parenting books. Share titles of the best with your librarian.

All parents need our support and assistance in order to fulfill their parenting role, just as schools need parents to help as their children learn. Be a true partner to the parents of your students!

Reflections

* Parent/teacher collaboration involves skills in both speaking and listening, essential elements in productive communication.

* Two essential elements in developing collaborative relationships between parents and teachers are trust and respect.

* The Parent-Teacher Conference provides a structured opportunity for parents and teachers to discuss mutual concerns and to work together.

* Teachers must plan, schedule and use a variety of ways to communicate with parents.

[11]LaMorte, Michael W., School Law: Cases and Concepts, Englewood Cliffs, NJ, Prentice Hall, 1990.

[12]Steele, Kathy, ***Involving Parents in Schools***, Beavercreek OH, Pieces of Learning, 1996.

Technology - A 21st Century Teaching Tool

When I am with my "80 something" father, he is a constant reminder of how much has changed in just one person's lifetime. My dad was born in 1913, before the start of World War I. He remembers electricity and telephone lines before they were commonplace in people's homes. He saw the first mass-produced cars and owned a Model A and a Model T Ford.

He remembers Lindbergh's flight across the Atlantic and tells about running outside when he heard a plane in the sky because this was such an unusual phenomenon. He lived in a time when a telegram came to deliver bad news and when people only made a long distance phone call in an emergency. He bought his first TV in the early 1950's, a black and white one with a 10" screen that appeared to weigh 100 pounds! He has used a manual typewriter all his life and

says he sees no reason to change now. I hope they keep manufacturing typewriter ribbons!

My parents still do not fly, don't have a microwave, VCR, car phone or personal computer, and don't use an ATM machine. They do have a color TV, a phone and a 1995 car. My dad is a master at using the remote control and can "channel surf" as quickly as anyone I know!

In many ways, my parents remind me of how schools have embraced technology... We've done something with it, but for the most part we go on functioning just like we have always done.

The world is changing quickly from the Industrial Age to the Information Age. This change is just as significant as the change that the Renaissance brought to the world over 500 years ago, but is at a much more rapid pace. Imagine being a teacher of calligraphy to a group of scribes during the Renaissance, at the time Gutenberg invented the printing press. You may have been the best teacher any scribe ever had, but what you were teaching would eventually become obsolete, for with books in mass production the world would no longer need scribes.

The book-based changes that began with Gutenberg's invention in the 1400's basically went unchanged for centuries. Then the 20th Century — my parents' century — dawned. This was the century for change, significant change, in just one lifetime.

An Era of Rapid Change

Our Information Age technology reinvents itself with startling rapidity. In the 1980s I worked as a training coordinator with an educational television station. My job involved visiting schools and designing workshops to help teachers use instructional television in their classrooms. At that time, I saw the typical equipment in most schools—one or two black and white TV's, sometimes a reel-to-reel videotape recorder, and a TV antenna on the roof. Few schools had access to cable or satellite dishes. If someone had asked me about improving their productivity by using a desktop or laptop personal computer, I would not have known what they were talking about!

Now personal computers are fairly commonplace, and the new technologies I am hearing about include:

• Information highways

• The Internet and on-line services

• Virtual communities

• Palm sized wireless devices

• Laptops capable of multimedia productions

• Virtual reality headsets

• Voice driven computers

• Web sites on World Wide Web

Technology in Education

But what has happened in schools during the coming of the Information Age? For decades the prediction has been that technology would transform our classrooms. However, certain technologies have found their niche in education, but schools have been much less changed by technology than the worlds of business, entertainment and communications.

In general, schools tend to be at least 10 years behind business and industry in their use of technology. Consider these questions:

What if we moved all the computers out of schools tomorrow?

Would it make a big difference in what students learn, how they learn it or the way schools function?

For some schools it would make a big difference. But for most schools in America, the effect would be only on the functions of the school office, not individual classrooms, to the extent that it would be difficult for work to continue.

Yet, if we removed all computers from businesses in our country, almost all would find it impossible to function. Even retail outlets are severely crippled when the computers are shut down. Recently I went to a video store to rent a movie. A thunderstorm came up and the electricity went out. All of the store's business came to a halt, for the entire video rental system was computerized.

Businesses have been building electronic highways while most of us in education have been using technological dirt roads! Why has this been the case? This is partly due to the person-to-person nature of education itself. Our "products," after all, are human beings. Because of this, education is a unique business. Yet our mission is to educate students today to function in the world of tomorrow when all of our training to do this immense task took place yesterdays...or yesteryears ago.

Much of what today's students are exposed to did not even exist when we went to school, and much of what they will face in the future we have yet to invent!

The Impact of Change

What does this mean to us as educators? In one word — CHANGE! Rapid change will be the one constant, the defining theme, the way of life in the 21st century. Many changes have already occurred. We have replaced 16 millimeter film projectors with VCRs and now to some extent with laser discs. Overheads are slowly giving way to computer projection panels. We have computer labs and computer classes, and we now update card catalogs into computerized databases.

Yes, this is change, but the changes that must occur to truly prepare our stu-

dents for the 21st Century must be much more drastic. They must fundamentally change the way we teach. The technology used in education needs to resemble the technology students are beginning to use and interact with in other parts of their lives.

Technology is not THE solution to education's problems, but it can be a catalyst for positive change to occur.

The meaningful use of technology in schools must go far beyond dropping a computer or VCR in the classroom. We need to discover new functions for technology in our schools, not merely ask how technology can help us do the things we already do. If we just continue to do what we have always done, just on a computer rather than in another low-tech way, we'll generally find that it increases our workload rather than enhancing our productivity. Consider these facts:

- By the year 2000, desktop personal computers will be as powerful as the super computers of the early 1990's.

- New technologies make it possible to transfer data at lightning speed and to combine text, sound and video images.

- The "information superhighway" allows for the transfer of information along fiber optic lines. This, in turn allows for the merging of a variety of information technologies.[13]

Recently, we've seen how the communications, cable and entertainment industries are merging. For example, Disney has purchased ABC. Turner Broadcasting has merged with Times Warner. And so it goes. This brings many implications for the home entertainment market, but the educational applications are limitless as well.

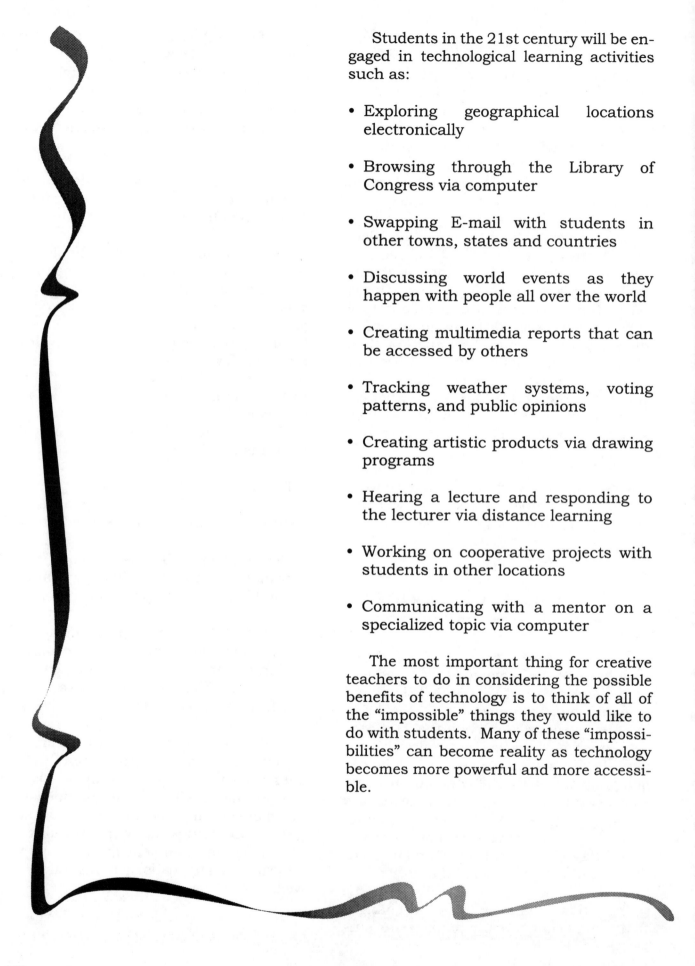

Students in the 21st century will be engaged in technological learning activities such as:

- Exploring geographical locations electronically

- Browsing through the Library of Congress via computer

- Swapping E-mail with students in other towns, states and countries

- Discussing world events as they happen with people all over the world

- Creating multimedia reports that can be accessed by others

- Tracking weather systems, voting patterns, and public opinions

- Creating artistic products via drawing programs

- Hearing a lecture and responding to the lecturer via distance learning

- Working on cooperative projects with students in other locations

- Communicating with a mentor on a specialized topic via computer

The most important thing for creative teachers to do in considering the possible benefits of technology is to think of all of the "impossible" things they would like to do with students. Many of these "impossibilities" can become reality as technology becomes more powerful and more accessible.

Technology - A 21st Century Teaching Tool

Teacher Reflection Page

1. What are some ways I have used technology in my teaching?

2. What successes have I had with technology?

3. What problems have I encountered?

4. What additional uses do I see for technology in my present teaching situation?

5. What could I do with technology in the future that is not possible for me to do now without it?

6. What scares or concerns me about technology?

Educational Applications for Technology

There are limitless ways to use technology to help us educate our students. Six specific ways to enhance educational objectives and outcomes through technology are discussed below. These applications overlap and are connected to one another. However, it will be helpful to look at them as separate entities so we can see more clearly the ways we can use technology to help us carry out our central mission of educating children.

1. Individualize instruction

With a multitude of technological resources, the curriculum can become much more individualized, fluid and personalized. No longer will the curriculum be driven solely by predigested print materials and texts. Teachers will be able to prescribe individual learning paths for students who then could move through the lessons at their own pace. Students will no longer be dependent on studying something or doing drill and practice exercises because this is the time in the calendar when all students do this activity. No longer will students be tied to a certain grade level of work when that level is either too hard or too easy.

Students will be able to create their own individualized curriculum through their own choices of resources. Lest we think this is nothing but a rosy future, it's important to realize that in such a scenario the problem becomes one of guidance. Without guidance from competent, information savvy teachers, students may flounder aimlessly for hours looking at snippets of information as they "surf the net" without really getting anything accomplished. Even worse, without appropriate teacher guidance and oversight, they may spend their time looking for and at garbage. In fact, one dilemma of the Information Age is that there's so much information it's often hard to find what you want when you want it. That is where the teacher comes in — as the facilitator and guide to students as they become the information retrievers.

We've given lip service to individualized instruction in education for a long time. Technology will give us the chance finally to really implement this strategy on a large scale.

But this means teachers must be willing to change. Technology-rich classrooms will not have desks in straight rows with the teacher in front. Textbooks and lectures will not be the major format for information gathering or new learning. Teachers will be able to truly individualize instruction but this means the role of the teacher will be quite different.

2. Help students become independent researchers, critical thinkers and problem solvers

Access to technology greatly enhances students' capacity to do basic research. When students use on-line tools, databases and resources, they are much more able to gather and evaluate information. When this happens, teachers should begin to see student research projects that are much more thorough and in depth. When students can routinely go on-line for information, there will be no excuse for outdated or incomplete information. Of course, kids will always be kids, so look for new excuses such as, *"The electricity was out so I couldn't do my homework!"*

Productivity tools such as databases, computer graphics and multimedia authoring programs will allow students to organize, analyze, interpret, develop and evaluate their own work. In other words, using these technological tools will help them learn to be independent problem solvers. Here are examples:

- Picture a math class where students collaboratively solve problems, exchange homework, and critique one another's answers. This is a very different scenario from the typical "Let me copy your math homework" attitude we see in so many schools today.

- Consider a class where groups of students build HyperCard stacks to demonstrate problem solving techniques and abstract concepts in many subject areas or in interdisciplinary work.

- Imagine a science class that downloads visual images from satellites and up to the minute scientific data is accessed on-line from government agencies. Then picture students developing hypotheses and solving problems based on this information. One class tracked the paths of all the hurricanes during the volatile 1995 hurricane season using digital satellite images and National Weather Service maps that were available on-line.

The three examples above are but a small sampling of how classrooms across America today use technology. The future will hold even more for student researchers and problem solvers.

3. Increase the quality and quantity of student writing and student products

More and more, students will use technology to prepare multimedia projects and presentations. A student doing a research project, for example, will be able to create a report using text, graphics, sound and video. This is a far cry from the reports of old copied directly from the encyclopedia!

Once this multimedia report is completed, a student will be able to present it to his or her class or another group of interested people or will be able to store it in a computerized student library for others to use in the future.

I've heard much concern about the quality of student writing. Technology can be an immense help in this area. Word processors reduce the phobia some students associate with writing. Technological tools can reduce students' frustration with poor handwriting, grammar and spelling. With such tools, editing and revising written work can be done more quickly and with ease. And the finished product can look great, just as good as something that is ready to be published professionally.

With a few more technological tools, artistic expression can be nurtured as part of the writing process. Student reports can be enhanced using video cameras, animation tools, scanners, digital photography, AutoCAD drawings, and sound digitizers. This technology will be especially helpful for those students who traditionally have problems in verbal and written communication.

Does this sound like a far-fetched dream? One hundred years ago students came to school with a slate tablet and a piece of chalk. The books, pencils, pens, notebooks, highlighters, calculators, and paper carried by today's students would have seemed an impossible dream in 1890. In the not too distant future, I predict that a portable computer with built in modem will be part of the school supplies of the average student.

4. Connections with the "real world"

Technology has the potential to allow students to take part in activities and projects that blur the distinction between school and the "real world" as we often call the world outside. When this happens, instead of working on hypothetical problems out of a textbook, students can go on-line and work on the same real life problems other students, or even adults out there in the "real world," are struggling with. They may participate in problem solving directly or through simulations, much as this type of activity is done in the workplace.

Helping students share their information and their solutions with others in this way becomes a major step in facilitating their interaction with others outside the four walls of the classroom. Many schools have students involved in creating a Web page for their class or their school. Students report that many school alumni visit their Web pages to find out what is going on in their Alma mater!

Telecommunications technology can give students opportunities to work with mentors outside school. Being linked to a mentor in the "real world" via the Internet or an on-line service is a cost effective and exciting way to match students and adults with similar interests.

Technology also can provide a "real world" audience for student work. As our students become linked to the world outside the classroom, their motivation to write and to complete research and other projects will soar. After all, real people "out there" will be seeing it!

5. Cooperative learning and communication all over the globe

Computers encourage far more collaboration among students in the classroom itself. As students work together, teachers learn to alter the physical set up of their rooms and modify daily schedules to give students more time to collaborate on projects.

Technology also allows cooperative learning to occur at a distance. Students can team up with students in another school, city, state or country to work together on a joint project or just to swap E-mail.

- During the Persian Gulf War, for example, a group of students in New York traded E-mail messages with students in Israel. Through this, the New York students got information on breaking events in the war as they occurred.

Technological tools allow students to inexpensively and instantly reach around the world, learning first hand about other cultures.

- Recently a group of high school students in Massachusetts participated in a distance learning session via a satellite hookup with students in Japan. Students on both sides of the globe could see one another on TV and ask each other questions on all kinds of issues.

- Thousands of students all over the United States took an interactive field trip to Kenya last spring. Sponsored by Turner Educational Services and narrated by a CNN reporter, this electronic field trip allowed students to participate in a live, interactive broadcast from Lake Nakunu National Park in Kenya, talk to experts about ecological problems in Africa and in their own communities, and even meet some Kenyan students who showed them how to make sounds like African animals!

174

Interactive satellite broadcasts such as these that link students not just via the written word, but also through sound and video, are powerful tools for student motivation and learning. Like these two groups of students who have now electronically visited Japan and Kenya, students in the 21st century will routinely link to all parts of the globe. The results of these interactions will be much more understanding of world problems and of those things that link us all into a "global village."

6. Access to interactive distance learning

Technology is opening new ways to learn and a broad range of subject areas to more students. Distance learning via satellite transmission is very different from the old "talking head" we often saw instructional television use years ago. Instead, it is a new way to deliver information and to give students and teachers access to high level, high interest courses and experiences. They can interact with the instructor and with other students, yet remain in a local setting.

For too long, educators based instructional opportunities for students on what the local school could provide. Higher level courses were often only available in large, wealthy schools or school districts. Interactive distance learning changes all of that. Many more courses will be available to students and also to teachers. Can you imagine getting a master's degree via distance learning courses available in your local school or even in your own home? Technology now makes this possible.

In the electronic learning system of the 21st century, students may listen to a teacher's presentation over television and have access to two-way audio and video systems that allow them to ask questions. We have used television as a teaching tool for decades, but the interactive quality of this new approach is its most important feature.

As one high school student who was taking a televised high school physics course complained, *"I have questions while the teacher is talking. But we're supposed to hold our questions until the once-a-week physics lab. By then, I don't even remember what the question was about! I'm lost if I can't ask my questions as we go along."* In an interactive distance learning system, this student could ask his questions right away.

Distance learning arrangements between grade levels and schools will become much more commonplace. It will not be unusual for a 4th grader, for instance, to take 7th grade math via a distance learning hookup.

Educational Applications for Technology

Teacher Reflection Page

I think most of us will agree that new technologies sound wonderful and hold lots of promise for education. But of course, as with anything else there are problems to be overcome. Educational leaders, such as district and school based administrators, need to consider these problems and concerns. Write your reflections and thoughts about the questions below. Share your answers and your concerns with your colleagues. Finally, it is essential that teachers ask these questions to the administrators and decision makers in the school district.

1. How are teachers going to be supported through the significant instructional shifts caused by technology?

2. How are teachers going to be trained so that they are comfortable with and competent in using these new technologies?

3. When are phone lines, fiber optic cable lines, modems, a reasonable number of computers, and other basic technological tools going to be installed in every classroom?

4. How are we going to deal with the significant differences in computer literacy and computer access between the "haves and the have nots" in our student population?

176

Final Thoughts about Technology

Technology can cause major educational changes. It can facilitate:

- Working in teacher teams

- Planning and teaching across the disciplines

- Modifying school schedules to accommodate ambitious class projects

- Integrating several different kinds of media

Using technology can also significantly change the way you teach. As one high school teacher said:

"As you work into using the computer in the classroom, you start questioning everything you have done in the past and wonder how you can adapt it to the computer. Then you start questioning the whole concept of what you originally did. Eventually you learn to undo your old way of thinking."

The array of technological tools for acquiring information and for thinking and expression allows more children more ways to enter the learning environment and succeed. These same things will provide the skills that will enable students to live productive lives in the global, digital information future of the 21st Century.

Do not underestimate the catalytic impact of technology. It can change the inertia and disinterest so often found in the traditional classroom. It has the potential to:

- Encourage fundamentally different forms of interaction among and between students and between students and teachers;

- Engage students systematically in higher-order cognitive tasks;

- Prompt teachers to question old assumptions about instruction and learning.

As we enter the technological Information Age, the teacher's role may become more and more "high touch" as many other tasks formerly done by teachers become "high tech." Technology, then, can replace (or reposition), but not replace, the teacher. Many of those routine tasks now done by teachers can be reassigned to technology, leaving the teacher in a new place educationally to do the things teachers really should be doing in the first place. Teachers will be freed to do the work that requires human interaction, continuous assessment, and improving the learning environment. These tasks include:

- Building strong, positive relationships with students

- Motivating students to love learning

- Facilitating the retrieval and understanding of all kinds of information

- Identifying and meeting students' emotional needs

- Developing student communities and teams for higher level thinking and problem solving

To see students so engaged in learning that they lose track of time; to see students so excited about learning that they come to school early and stay late; and to see educators who have time to develop strong relationships with their students and who can meet their individual needs ... This is the hope technology gives us.

At best, technology will allow us to fulfill age-old dreams. With it we can individualize instruction. We can enhance student learning through simulations and distance learning. We can take them to new places and introduce them to the "real world." We can give them the tools to create, to write, to do research, and to communicate.

At worst we will use the technology to help us do the same things we've always done. Go back and reread the other chapters in this book. As you do, reflect upon them in light of the many possibilities technology may hold. Technology could well be the key that will open the door to the many other teaching tools for the 21st century.

Reflections

* We live in an era of rapid technological change.

* New technologies are beginning to have an impact on what happens in the classroom and this impact will grow exponentially in the 21st century.

* Technology will allow us to teach in many more innovative and exciting ways and will allow our students to engage in a variety of new learning activities.

* There are limitless educational applications for technology, but all require teacher planning, imagination and creativity.

* In an age of "high tech" teachers will be needed more and more for "high touch" work with students that requires human interaction, continuous assessment, counseling, and directing or facilitating learning.

* We need to find a way to deal with significant differences in computer literacy and computer access between the "haves" and the "have nots" of the Information Age.

[13] O'Neil, John, "Using Technology to Support Authentic Learning," ASCD Update, Vol. 35, Number 8, October 1993.

Bibliography

ASCD Update, Volume 35, Number 5, June, 1993.

ASCD Update, Volume 35, Number 8, October, 1993.

Armstrong, Thomas. *Multiple Intelligences in the Classroom*. Alexandria, Virginia: Association for Supervision and Curriculum Development, 1994.

Balsamo, Kathy. *Thematic Activities for Student Portfolios*. Beavercreek, Ohio: Pieces of Learning, 1994.

Barbe, Walter and Raymond H Swassing. *Teaching Through Modality Strengths*. Columbus, Ohio: Zaner-Bloser Inc.,1980.

Blenk, Katie and Doris Landau Fine. *Making School Inclusion Work: A Guide to Everyday Practices*. Cambridge, Massachusetts: Brookline Books, 1995.

Caine, Renate and Geoffrey. *Making Connections: Teaching and the Human Brain*. Alexandria, Virginia: ASCD, 1991.

Chapman, Carolyn. *If the Shoe Fits*. Palatine, Illinois: IRI/Skylight Publishing, Inc., 1993.

Clark, Barbara. *Growing Up Gifted*. 4th ed. New York: Macmillan Publishing Company, 1992.

Cohen, Philip. "Understanding the Brain," *Education Update* Vol. 37, Number 7, Alexandria, Virginia: ASCD, September, 1995.

Coil, Carolyn. *Becoming an Achiever: A Student Guide*. Beavercreek, Ohio: Pieces of Learning, 1994.

Coil, Carolyn. *Motivating Underachievers: 172 Strategies for Success*. Beavercreek, Ohio: Pieces of Learning, 1992.

Costa, A., Bellanca, J., & Fogarty, R. *If Minds Matter*. Palatine, Illinois: IRI/Skylight Publishing, Inc., 1992.

Cox, June, Neil Daniel, and Bruce O. Boston. *Educating Able Learners*. Austin, Texas: University of Texas Press, 1985.

Education Update. Volume 37, Number 6, Alexandria, Virginia: ASCD, August, 1995.

Education Update. Volume 37, Number 9, Alexandria, Virginia: ASCD, December, 1995.

Educational Leadership. Volume 51, Number 8, Alexandria, Virginia: ASCD, May, 1994.

Educational Leadership. Volume 52, Number 8, Alexandria, Virginia: ASCD, May, 1995.

Educational Leadership. Volume 53, Number 2, Alexandria, Virginia: ASCD, October, 1995.

Electronic Learning. January/February, 1996.

Friend, Marilyn and Lynne Cooke. "Inclusion." *Instructor*, New York: November/December 1993.

Gallagher, Patricia A. *Teaching Students with Behavior Disorders: Techniques and Activities for Classroom Instruction*. Denver, Colorad: Love Publishing Co., 1988.

Gardner, Howard. *Frames of Mind*. New York: Basic Books, 1983.

Gardner, Howard. "Reflections on Multiple Intelligences: Myths and Messages."

Phi Delta Kappan. Volume 77, Number 3, November 1995.

Gibbs, Nancy. "The E.Q. Factor." *Time Magazine,* October 2, 1995.

Henry, Gertrude. *Cultural Diversity Awareness Inventory.* Hampton, Virginia: ERIC Document #ED282657.

Hilliard, Gerri. "Ability Grouping Expert Sounds A Warning: An Interview with Karen Rogers." Georgia Supporters for the Gifted Newsletter, Winter, 1993.

Johnson, David W. and Roger T. *Reducing School Violence Through Conflict Resolution.* Alexandria, Virginia: ASCD, 1995.

Johnson, Nancy. *The Faces of Gifted.* Beavercreek, Ohio: Pieces of Learning, 1989.

La Morte, Michael W. *School Law: Cases and Concepts.* Englewood Cliffs, New Jersey: Prentice Hall, 1990.

Nicolau, S. and C.L. Ramos. *You're a Parent...and You're a Teacher, Too.* New York: Hispanic Policy Development Project. ERIC Document #335173, 1990.

Perrone, Vito, ed. *Expanding Student Assessment.* Alexandria, Virginia: ASCD, 1991.

Research Bulletin, No. 11. *Phi Delta Kappa Center for Evaluation, Development and Research,* Bloomington, Indiana: May, 1993.

Riche, Martha Farnsworth. "We're All Minorities Now." *American Demographics,* October 1991.

Sisk, Dorothy. *Creative Teaching of the Gifted.* New York: McGraw-Hill, Inc., 1987.

Steele, Kathy. *Involving Parents in Schools.* Beavercreek Ohio: Pieces of Learning, 1996.

Time Magazine, Special Issue, Fall 1993.

U.S. Department of Education, Office of Educational Research and Improvement. *National Excellence: A Case for Developing America's Talent.* Washington, D.C.: U.S. Government Printing Office October, 1993.

U.S. Department of Health, Education and Welfare. *Education of the Gifted and Talented, Marland Report to the Congress of the United States.* Washington, D.C.: U.S. Government Printing Office, 1972.

Whelage, Gary G. and Robert A. Rutter. "Dropping Out: How Much Do Schools Contribute to the Problem?" *Teachers College Record,* Spring 1986.

Wiggins, Grant. *Assessing Student Performance: Exploring the Purposes and Limits of Testing.* San Francisco: Jossey-Bass Publishers, 1993.

Wiles, Jon and Joseph Bondi. *Curriculum Development: A Guide to Practice.,* 4th ed. Columbus, Ohio: Merrill Publishing Company, 1992.

Willis, Scott. *Curriculum Update.* Alexandria, Virginia: ASCD, September,1993.

Willis, Scott. "Making Schools More Inclusive." *Curriculum Update,* Alexandria, Virginia: ASCD, October, 1994.

Winebrenner, Susan. *Teaching Gifted Kids in the Regular Classroom.* Minneapolis, Minnesota: Free Spirit Publishing, 1992.

Appendix

Blank Lesson Plan Format for Multiple Intelligences

Naturalist Intelligence

INDIVIDUAL LESSON PLAN - MULTIPLE INTELLIGENCES

ACTIVITIES - STUDENT CHOICES

Visual/Spatial	Verbal/Linguistic

Bodily/Kinesthetic	Logical/Mathematical

Student Choices in Ways to Learn
Visual/Spatial _____

Bodily/Kinesthetic _____

Verbal/Linguistic _____

Logical/Mathematical _____

Optional
Student-Parent
Cooperative Activity

Required Activities Teacher's Choice	Product/Performance Required	Assessment Required Activities

Product/Performance Student Choice	Assessment Student Choice

©1997 Carolyn Coil and Pieces of Learning

INDIVIDUAL LESSON PLAN - MULTIPLE INTELLIGENCES

ACTIVITIES - STUDENT CHOICES

Required Activities
Teacher's Choice

Product/Performance
Required

Assessment
Required Activities

Optional
Student-Parent
Cooperative Activity

Product/Performance
Student Choice

Assessment
Student Choice

Student Choices in
Ways to Learn

Interpersonal
_____

Intrapersonal
_____

Musical/Rhythmic
_____

Naturalist
_____

Interpersonal

Intrapersonal

Musical/Rhythmic

Naturalist

Naturalist Intelligence

When Gardner first wrote about the multiple intelligences, he indicated that there were probably more than the seven he originally identified. Recently he has identified an eighth intelligence, the Naturalist Intelligence. It is another Object Related intelligence.

The ability to discern, identify, organize and classify plants and animals; includes a keen sense of observation and the ability to seek, obtain and put order to information about the natural world. These skills can be extended and applied in the non-natural world as well.

Eleven year old Clay has a name his mother says fits him perfectly. He loves the out-of-doors and prefers activities that keep him close to nature and the land. In school he excels in earth sciences. On weekend camping trips with his scout troop, he can identify almost every plant or animal anyone sees. Each summer, Clay spends a month with his grandparents at the ocean. Here he has amassed a collection of more than five hundred shells. He classifies them in a variety of ways and enjoys making up new categories that are different from the ones he finds in books. Clay has a strong naturalist intelligence.

Characteristics:

- involves the ability to recognize flora and fauna

- makes distinctions, comparisons and contrasts between and among things in the natural world

- oriented toward enjoying outdoor life

- includes the ability to live off the land

- feels comfortable with nature and the natural world

- can create categories and sort and index items accordingly

- organizes in a way that explains and makes things more understandable

Representative Products:

- ✓ Science projects
- ✓ Charts
- ✓ Experiments
- ✓ Collections of objects
- ✓ Shadow box

Representative Activities:

- ✓ Build a school nature trail
- ✓ Conduct experiments and categorize data
- ✓ Create categories to classify information in all subject areas
- ✓ Take a field trip to a nature preserve
- ✓ Use memorization techniques based on putting items in categories
- ✓ Read stories about out-of-door adventures

Representative Careers:

- ✓ Zoologist
- ✓ Zookeeper
- ✓ Fisherman
- ✓ Agricultural experimenter
- ✓ Environmental scientist
- ✓ Biological researcher
- ✓ Park ranger
- ✓ Wilderness tour guide